TIME C̶ ̶ ̶ ̶E
LAST GOAL

This book is for all the little boys and girls who grew up loving hockey and for whatever reasons can only play it in their minds for the rest of their lives. This is also for my grandfather, Bill Miller, who loved the game, ...and for my daughter Katie who stands beside me in the blue and white.

"Plan the parade." — Ubiquitous sarcastic remark directed at Toronto hockey fans when they get their hopes up.

TIME OF THE LAST GOAL
WHY HOCKEY IS OUR GAME

*To Tanya, Taylor and Jaylynn —
with all good wishes —
Go Leafs Go!*

Bruce Meyer

BRUCE MEYER

Copyright © 2014 Bruce Meyer

Meyer, Bruce, 1957-, author
    Time of the last goal : why hockey is our game / Bruce Meyer.

ISBN 978-0-88753-512-3 (pbk.)

1. Hockey--Canada. 2. Hockey--Social aspects--Canada.
3. Meyer, Bruce, 1957-. I. Title.

GV848.4.C3M49 2014   796.9620971   C2014-903738-4

Cover photo by William Melton, courtesy of Shutterstock
Design & Layout: Jason Rankin
Editor: Marty Gervais, Meghan Desjardins, Vanessa Shields

Published by Black Moss Press at 2450 Byng Road, Windsor, Ontario, N8W 3E8. Canada. Black Moss books are distributed in Canada and the U.S. by Fitzhenry & Whiteside. All orders should be directed there.

    Fitzhenry & Whiteside
    195 Allstate Parkway
    Markham, ON
    L3R 4T8

Black Moss Press
EST. 1969

Black Moss would like to acknowledge the generous financial support from both the Canada Council for the Arts and the Ontario Arts Council.

ONTARIO ARTS COUNCIL
CONSEIL DES ARTS DE L'ONTARIO
50 YEARS OF ONTARIO GOVERNMENT SUPPORT OF THE ARTS
50 ANS DE SOUTIEN DU GOUVERNEMENT DE L'ONTARIO AUX ARTS

Canada Council   Conseil des arts
for the Arts   du Canada

CONTENTS

The Arena   10
Game Day   12
Johnny Bower   16
National Anthem: Road Hockey   17

FIRST PERIOD   19
The Parade to Forever   20
I Say the Walls Shall Crumble Down   29
First Intermission: Skating   31

SECOND PERIOD   37
The Buds on My Grandparents' Maple Tree   38
The Maple Leaf Forever   54
Second Intermission: The Surly Bonds of Earth   56

THIRD PERIOD   67
The Quest   68
The Parade   82

SUDDEN DEATH OVERTIME   83
Arent Arentsz's "Skaters on the Amstel," 1625   84
Time of the Last Goal   85

Acknowledgements   95
About the Author   95

SERVICE

for my father

Snowbound nights at the roofless rink
we would be called in our wet wool
to the dressing room for chalk-talk,
and after a coaching the snowfall

would be gone, the ice smooth again,
as if shovelled by angels. One night
the door swung wide in the wind when
I saw my father, a drop of silver bright

on the tip of his nose, raise a shovelful
and dump flakes and shavings overboard.
I had not noticed he was there at all.
In a rush, I rarely see the good around

me. Hands that have wrought miracles
never applaud themselves, their labours
fibred in the spirit of love that reveals
our needs and their simple answers.

INTRODUCTION:

My mentor, Northrop Frye, always said that if you want to understand the psyche of a nation you should look at its epics — the poetry that celebrates what is great and important about a nation. The imaginary vision that a people create for themselves resides in the great events they choose to celebrate or lament. As a collective statement for what a nation believes, the epic reveals a national identity in all its glory and foibles. Alas, no one has written a hockey epic, yet. My corollary to Frye's statement is that if you want to understand the emotional dynamic of a people, their passions and their undiscovered drives, you should look at what they consider their most important sport.

    This book, *Time of the Last Goal*, is my attempt to look into the Canadian imagination and, in some way, explain why hockey is our national sport. As much as I adore Canadians, I am puzzled by them. I love the history of this nation, but more than just loving its history I am fascinated by the question of why we do what we do. As someone who has taught Canadian literature at various post-secondary institutions, I am troubled by the absence of tragedy in our national canon. Mature literatures have tragedies. E.J. Pratt attempted epic poems such as "Brebeuf and His Bretheren," where his goal was to identify what is unique about us as a nation. Those poems, beautiful and intriguing as they are, are now slightly dated and are, alas, often left off course reading lists. For his final poem, Pratt was faced with a tough decision. He could write about the Franklin Expedition of 1848 and its tragic consequences or he could chronicle the building of the CPR. Both topics were about man's struggle with nature. Unwell at the time, Pratt chose to sit in the scenic car of national dream's railway and watch the mountains. He avoided tragedy.

    There have been countless stories of tragic figures in our national consciousness who have been associated with hockey. Their stories, however, have not really been told. The hockey fraternity, like soldiers, keeps mum about those players who fell on hard times and never rose above them. Such stories are lacunal to us. They are there, but they are buried in our hockey lore. They are the stories we try to avoid when we dream about hockey and recite the narratives of its memorable moments. That said, I have to remind myself and my readers that hockey does not happen completely on the ice. It is a game of the mind, a game of dreams and the imagination as much as it is a game between players who battle for possession of a puck. It is a game that also takes place in the time between the games — those long hours when the hockey lover pours over statistics or constructs his fantasy team. The game lives in those pauses when the snow is falling and anticipation for the next set of tickets or the next broadcast transforms itself into an imaginative landscape where metaphors guide the plays, where the struggle between your team and the other team becomes an eschatological battle between good and evil…even though in hockey the game is "the good old hockey game" and there is no white shirt and no dark shirt, just the players and the plays they make.

At the root of the way we perceive hockey is an imaginative driver or engine that constantly reminds us of what we should celebrate even though we are not sure why. I have long wrestled with the question of why hockey is important to us. I am certain now that the imaginative force that brings us to the game of hockey and asks that we love the game as part of our national consciousness is the same spirit that makes our history, our literature, and our perspective on the world unique among nations. Yes, other nations love hockey, but I assert that their love of hockey is different. To them it is a sport. To us hockey is almost a religion. This book is an attempt to explain why, at least from a personal perspective, we have chosen to make hockey our game.

Hockey is the ubiquitous expression of our national mentality. It is a violent sport but we are not a violent people. It a sport that ties us to our most ferocious season. Our climate is one of extremes, and winter is the most ferocious of those extreme seasons. We celebrate that ferocity by shooting pieces of frozen rubber at one hundred kilometres an hour or more at a man in a mask in the hope that he will not stop the projectile. We hurt each other by slamming our opponents' bodies into solid walls, yet we also shake hands at the end of a playoff series in a beautiful act of sportsmanship and forgiveness.

That season is our time to pursue one goal and one goal only: the goal of having our team of choice crowned as champions of the ice joust, and we are not completely satisfied with ourselves or with our chosen champions until we have achieved that one perfect, final goal of raising the Stanley Cup and watching the players drink from it in a moment of secular communion. In that moment, we project ourselves onto those players — even moreso if they are our chosen representatives in the quest for hockey's grail — and when we watch them drink from the great silver chalice we are redeemed from the purgatory of waiting for next year. We vicariously become the knights who quested after the Holy Grail and we long for that moment when we achieve that one, perfect, final goal that can redeem us and name us as champions.

B.M.

THE ARENA

On those brittle, mid-December nights
before the local Kiwanis members raised
enough money to put a roof sturdily
over the local rink, tweed-coated fathers
would appear during short game breaks
to shovel clean the snowied silver ice.

That smell of wet wool crusted with ice
and the sour milk breath of boy knights
crescendoed in white clouds. The heart breaks
recalling them there: so many hopes raised
higher than stars, the sons, the fathers
dreaming of a love unattainable, sturdily

shouldering wintry desires and sturdily
building legends of the mind in layered ice.
Realities melt when spring comes. Fathers
should know better. The boys spend nights
on numbing rinks, toes dead, arms raised
in triumph holding aloft a grail that breaks

the hearts of heroes. A rookie winger breaks
in alone. No one breathes. The goalie sturdily
stands his ground. This is a nation raised
on the possibilities in a wrist shot. Open ice
always ahead, limitless as clear starry nights
transfixed by a TV glow, sons and fathers

living for the comeback that grandfathers
a lost cause into tomorrow, and finally breaks
the silence with a goal waved off. Nights
like this are certainties in those sturdily
indefatigable back street homes where the ice
is a blanket wrapping itself up to raised

porches and sometimes the sills. I was raised
in the silver blade-cut of such love where fathers
made their marks on winters past. The ice
yawns like an empty net. The shooter breaks
in and fires wide. This pain, such pain, sturdily
shakes the core of my soul on such nights

when I raised my hopes too high. Hope breaks
like an icicle a father's shovel knocks sturdily
from eaves, ice shattering the silence of still nights.

GAME DAY

I needed to get downtown from St. George and Bloor to pick up my daughter at her daycare before the light went out of the late afternoon. I dislike going home in darkness. I scrambled over a snow bank — that Berlin Wall between the foot race and the rest of the journey — and waved my arms to hail a cab. A Beck taxi pulled over and I slid, then fell, down the outer slope toward the vehicle as I tried to balance my briefcase in one hand while grabbing hold of the cab with the other to avoid falling under the wheels. The driver turned in his seat and opened the back door.

I told him I needed to go to Wellington and Front and brushed the grey smear of road salt from the sleeves of my black coat. He pulled forward and started the meter. We began our small talk — the weather, the traffic, the route from here to there. "I know your voice," he said. "I've heard it somewhere recently."

"I was on radio recently. CBC," I replied.

"That's where I heard you! You were talking about Sophocles. You're the Great Books guy with Michael Enright!"

"That's me." For the past several months in the winter of 1999, I had been appearing on CBC AM's *This Morning*. Enright played the pupil and I did the teacher's role to explain what the classics had to say and how they were still present in our lives and our culture. I had been discussing the great works of Western literature — the Bible, Dante, Homer, Virgil. The series was heard each morning, coast to coast, at 9:00 a.m.

The driver half turned in his seat. I started watching the road ahead. The traffic was moving slowly but we kept crossing intersections and he had only one eye on the lane. He was a balding, older man, perhaps in his sixties. He looked slightly haggard and his colour was borderline grey. His grey tweed coat was worn at the cuffs and his beige canvas work shirt was open at the neck. "Yeah, I've been listening to you. You've really inspired me."

His enthusiasm made me feel good. I had been hoping to take the message of the Great Books — often referred to as the dead books by many contemporary commentators — beyond the reaches of ivy-covered halls. He'd heard all the broadcasts in the series. "Which ones have caught your attention?" I asked.

"Sophocles!" he said as we stopped at a red light. "By the way, are you in a hurry?" I shook my head politely though, in fact, I was eager to get to the daycare. "I drive cab for a living, but my real passion, my real desire is to be a writer. I want to write a play — a tragedy to be precise. You don't mind if we pull off and I pick your brains for a few minutes do you?"

We soon found a side street not too far from Roy Thomson Hall, and he shut off the engine and turned off the meter. "My name's Al," he said.

"Al…what?"

"Al Smith. I used to be a goalie years ago…"

"You're Al Smith?" I asked incredulously. "Geez, Al, I met you when I was a kid. We were at the CNE. You were standing all by yourself at some makeshift booth an auto maker had set up in the Car Building one August morning. It was hotter than Hades and you were wearing a pale blue suit. I was the only one there so we talked for a long time. You signed my autograph book."

"Yeah, well, I guess I did a lot of those events. Weren't you with your mother and kid sister and grandmother?"

"That was me. That was me!"

"Yeah, I remember. So you don't mind if I ask you a few questions…Dr. Meyer?"

"Call me Bruce."

We sat in the cab for at least an hour. Part of the way through our discussion I asked if he was getting stiff from turning around. He waved it off. During the course of the conversation we talked about Sophocles' *Theban Plays* and the dark consequences of not knowing one's own identity. We talked about the *persona* in Classical drama — the masks that actors wore on stage in the very ritualized and solemn productions in order to become the character. I told him that Sophocles was probably the first playwright not to wear a *persona* because he was asthmatic and had a weak voice for the stage, kind of like Jacques Plante. Al nodded in deep thought.

Then, I linked the idea of the dramatic mask, the assumed identity, to the goalie mask.

"You're right. I've told people I'm Al Smith and they tell me that all they remember is what I had on my mask."

We covered Coleridge's essay on Hamlet, and ran through the thoughts of Nietzsche and the German philosopher's response to the concept of the high born and the low born — the *spoudaios* and the *phaulos* — in Aristotle's *Nichomachean Ethics*. Well into the conversation, I forgot that Al was a hockey player. I thought I was talking to a fellow poet or a literary colleague. I realized I was running late for my daughter just as we wrapped up our discussion of Arthur Miller's ground-breaking essay on tragedy that the American playwright had written in support of *Death of a Salesman*.

"Yeah, that makes sense," he said as he turned the key in the ignition. "That makes sense." As we pulled from the curb and back into traffic he remarked "I wanna pick your brains about Modern Poetry."

"That's my field."

"Well, I gotta talk to you about Sylvia Plath and Anne Sexton. Do you know anything about them?"

"I live and breathe them. Other than the fact they both committed suicide, they were both students at Harvard for a single winter term in a Creative Writing workshop run by Robert Lowell."

"No kidding?"

"If you want to understand the link between the two poets, look at Lowell and look at A. Alvarez's introduction to the Penguin anthology, *The New Poetry*. The essay is titled "Against the Gentility Principle," and Alvarez, who I met one evening at the Poetry Society in London, England, said that he always regretted writing that piece because it became a self-fulfilling prophecy."

"Yeah, I see that. But hell, didn't those two poets get a load of amazing writing done before they checked out? 'Panzer man, Panzer man…' I love that stuff. I'm writing a play about them."

"About Plath and Sexton?"

"Yep. Well, sort of. You wouldna thunk it, eh?"

"Hey Al, what do I owe you? You killed the meter."

"My pleasure Bruce. We gotta meet again soon. I'll look for you on Bloor Street."

We never did meet again. That's the tragedy. Al sent me an invitation to his play produced by the Alumni Theatre. It was titled "Confessions to Anne Sexton." I fell ill with pneumonia during its run. Al spent his Eagleson settlement money — money awarded to players who had been fleeced by a lawyer who was supposed to oversee their retirement fund — on the play. The production ran for the better part of a month, then closed down.

There was only one review, that by Toronto poet Kevin Connolly. Connolly noted that the production was a sad affair. A hockey player leaves his minor league team and travels across the northeast US to see a play about Plath and Sexton. Connolly concluded his review with the statement that there were more people on the stage than there were in the audience. Several months later, Al Smith passed away from pancreatic cancer. Canadian literary history does not speak of Al Smith's play. It was a tragedy, something we as a nation are not yet ready to embrace. The reason why is hockey.

JOHNNY BOWER

He could stop a train with that smile,
leaning into the play, blood trickling
in a meander scar across his vision,
his wooden sword sweep checking the crease.

His hair was what puzzled me most —
even in the third period with sweat
pouring off his forehead like tropical rain
his hair was always neatly slicked.

Never admitted his age; age was something
years could not pry out of him — he lived
and simply kept on tending having learned
if life fires horseshit at you, you stop it.

Stand up, he said to the world. Stay on your feet
through eons of minor league bus rides
and diesel fumes that fired his own engines.
Goalies are machines. They only look human.

NATIONAL ANTHEM: ROAD HOCKEY

The middle of my journey,
as the train shakes,
I wake from a dream
about my childhood
where I saw the boys
I played hockey with
on frozen streets
beneath purple dusks.
Snow had settled
On the brown furrows
of the fall ploughings
the way a dusting of ice
clung to our corduroys
as we shouted and raved
in a dead-end street,
pushing and hacking
each other's spindly legs
until the night descended
blackening the game
and called us home
to those tiny rooms
taped with clippings
of Howe and Hull
and silver grails.
I wanted to go back there,
wanted to dream again
of what I would become
but only became
the things I am

regardless of the dreams.
And as I woke just now,
at some point in a journey
I realized we'd all
become grown men
and the waking, not the growing
left me angry. Snow whirls
by the coach car window,
still clings to the furrows
of pant legs and fields
as the journeymen continue on
their battles of earthly overtime
and the sudden darkness
after.

FIRST PERIOD

THE PARADE TO FOREVER

Toronto has been reborn after a long winter. The grass is green again. The air is heavy with the first lilacs and apple blossoms that open in my grandmother's backyard. On the lawns of surrounding houses bright yellow forsythias look as if they are raising their arms to cheer for something, and they are not the only ones who are shouting their joy in the streets. I am five years old and the world to me is as perfect as it can be, perhaps because I have not yet learned what failure and defeat are and what they do to the heart.

The date is April 22, 1962. I am staying at my grandparents' house in North Toronto because my mother is about to have a baby, and I have been told the new sibling will arrive in time for my fifth birthday the next day. My grandmother has been at the doctor's all day with my mother.

I have spent the day running around with a neighbourhood boy who is a daredevil. I try to keep up. When my grandmother returns home, the boy is sent home. My grandfather tells her that the last straw was when he discovered the wild boy and I sitting on the crest of the verandah roof almost two stories up. I see my grandfather far below calling for me on the front walk of his house. He turns and staggers as if experiencing heart failure when he looks up and sees us perched on high. We wave to him and to startled passersby.

I am ordered to bed around 7:00 p.m. but not long after I am asleep I am awakened by my grandfather's yelp from downstairs. Something has happened. Perhaps the baby has come. No one comes to tell me any news. The rest of the night is stillness.

On the morning of my birthday, St. George's Day, I rise and learn the baby has not yet come. "We shall go to the park today," my grandmother offers over breakfast.

I ask my grandmother why my grandfather yelled in the night. "It was the game," she replied. "They won." I wasn't sure what she was talking about but take it at face value. The park seems more important.

The daffodils are out in Muir Park. The sunken garden carved into Burke Brook ravine is a tribute to the man who wrote the first Anglo-Canadian national anthem, "The Maple Leaf Forever."

There are shrubberies shaped in the form of animals. One is cut in the shape of a duck. City gardeners are turning over the beds in preparation for the planting that will come in the days ahead, and there is a scent of musky earth in the air — the scent of life and vitality. My grandmother and I make our way down a stone staircase and stand in front the memorial to Alexander Muir. It is set in a terraced hillside, an ornament of the surrounding gardens.

"Is someone buried in there?" I ask her in hushed tones as we stare at the stone plaque. She points to the words and the carved maple leaf above an inscription. I patiently read each word, say the familiar ones out loud, and stutter to pronounce the ones I don't. Above the solemn inscription is painted a brilliant orange and red and yellow maple leaf on the bas relief carving as if it is blazing with autumn glory and ready to be ironed between sheets of wax paper so it will last forever. Beneath the dedication are the words of a poem.

In days of yore
From Britain's shore
Wolfe the dauntless hero came

"Who is Wolfe, Nana?"

My grandmother's face takes on a stoic look with her chin raised and her lips pursed. She begins to sing "The Maple Leaf Forever."

"We have a record of it at home," she tells me as we wind our way out of the garden. "Let's have some lunch and listen to it. It is a song you need to learn."

A woman waves to us. It is Mrs. Young who lives in an apartment overlooking Muir Park. The two ladies stop and converse. Mrs. Young is tall, thin, and white-haired. She is far older than my grandmother. She tells us she is ninety-five. She looks at me and says "Do you know I am as old as Canada?" I do not know what to say.

"Do you like chocolates?" she asks as if still trying to draw me out. I nod that I do. For a moment I expect her to produce one for me.

That doesn't happen. "I am a great-granddaughter of Laura Secord," she announces with pride.

Mrs. Young invites my grandmother and I up to her apartment for some tea and Digestive biscuits (still no chocolates anywhere) and shows me a tiny silver photograph which she allows me to hold. The picture is of a very old woman, dressed in black, seated, and wearing a white cap with a frill around it. The eyes of the old woman in the picture are round and almost glazed like two marbles. She appears to be holding a white loaf of bread wrapped in a blanket. A small melon protrudes from the top of the bundle.

"That is me she is holding," says Mrs. Young as she makes her way to a chair and sits down. "That is my great-grandmother, Laura Secord, holding me just after I was born."

"You have looked into the eyes of Laura Secord," my grandmother says proudly on our way home for lunch. "When that old woman in the tin type was a young woman she saved Canada during the War of 1812. She told the British that the Americans were going to attack at Beaver Dam, and the red coats got there before the Americans and won the battle. That is why we are still here as a country." I am not impressed. There wasn't a chocolate in sight and I knew it was rude to ask if she had any.

We go back to my grandparents' house after tea with Mrs. Young and the shadowy image of the woman behind the almighty source of unlimited candy. As we sit at the white, cast-iron-topped kitchen table and eat our grilled cheese sandwiches, my grandmother decides to give me a history lesson about the War of 1812. She describes the bloody battle of Lundy's Lane near Niagara Falls when the Canadian militia fired through the fog and mowed down the British regulars by mistake and how the Canadians then had to face the Americans on their own through a long night of hand to hand fighting in a graveyard that soon received their mortal remains.

And as for Wolfe, he had red hair just like me. In another war that had been fought in Quebec he had defeated the French general Montcalm and claimed Canada for England. My grandmother reached into one of the kitchen drawers and produced a little Union Jack on a black rod and unrolled it. It had been sitting in the drawer since the Royal Visit of 1939. She waved it in the air.

Wolfe knew what was to come, she said, and as he rowed across the St. Lawrence River to the battle for Canada he read Thomas Gray's "Elegy in a Country Churchyard." "The paths of glory lead but to the grave," she said solemnly and shook her head. Both Wolfe and Montcalm, gallant generals that they were, died in the battle, but Wolfe's final words were 'Now that I have seen my victory let me die in peace.' We must go the Museum and see his hat. They have it there."

"Before I forget," my grandmother added, here is Muir's anthem. She rummaged through a stack of old records that sat on the bottom shelf of the dining room what-not. Through the scratch of years, the voices of men emerged. Their throats seemed strained as if they were singing through the sands of an hour glass. The record whirled at 78 rpm and I thought it would fly off the turn-table.

The singer's words were about planting Britannia's flag — the Union Jack like the one my grandmother said she waved every Victoria Day and July first — on Canada's "fair domain" and how it entwined other flowers: thistles, shamrocks, roses. My grandmother's face glowed as the singers broke into their refrain: "The Maple Leaf, our emblem dear, the Maple Leaf forever! God save our King and heaven bless, the Maple Leaf forever."

The second verse rang out about the battles "at Queenston Heights and Lundy's Lane" where "our brave fathers side by side, for freedom, home and loved ones dear firmly stood and nobly died." Before I could ask what they had died for, the song explained they had died for "those dear rights." I asked my grandmother what was mean by "those dear rights."

She smiled. "They are everything that allows you to be who you are."

On my grandmother's front lawn stands a very large, old maple tree that she and my grandfather planted shortly after they moved into the house in the early 1920s. The tree's arms reach over the street. In the spring it drips sap all over my father's car. He says, "The bugs will stick to it."

Every fall, the leaves turn a brilliant orange and red. They are the colours of passion and fire that fill everyone in the family with a determination not only to have the strength for the coming winter but to revel in the beauty of the season. Just before the cold rains come every year and the leaves fall, the tree turns blood red. My grandmother picks up the windfalls and spreads them around a vase of orange mums in the centre of the Thanksgiving dinner table. The song that I hear in my head is that distant, ethereal record of the first national anthem of English Canada. What was "forever" all about? Was it the promise of permanence, warmth, comfort, and love? Was it something that I was a part of? As my grandmother lays the meal on the table she says "this is our tradition." My eye is fixed on the read and orange leaves. They are the leaves that I saw open in the spring the day we went downtown to see the Maple Leafs' parade.

I am standing on my grandparent's front lawn, looking back at the house, and a newly opened maple leaf flutters above me on the tree, the first on its bough. We walk along Glengrove Avenue and catch a yellow and maroon bus at Yonge Street (I think the street is named for the old lady we met the day before). My grandmother takes me downtown on the red subway train from its terminus at Eglinton Station.

The baby has still not arrived.

At 10:00 a.m. as the Royal Ontario Museum opens its doors, we stride directly through the rotunda, me by the hand, into what had once been the Canadian gallery on the first floor. I would prefer to stop and look at the Medieval armour in the glass cases. There is a small, brass cannon sitting out by itself and I want to play with it, but my grandmother is on a mission. She walks up to a guard.

"Where is Wolfe's hat? I want to show my grandson because he is learning about Canadian history."

The guard looks puzzled and cranes his neck up and down the aisles as if he is trying to locate a lost memory that has suddenly become real again.

"I'm not sure, Ma'am. I'll go and ask."

A few minutes later the custodian reappears with a grey-haired, courtly-looking curator whose face is strained as if he is going to share some bad news with us.

"Madam," he says in hushed tones as if not wanting anyone else in the building to hear, "I'm afraid we no longer have Wolfe's hat."

"What do you mean?" my grandmother responds, startled and slightly confused. "It is one of your most valuable artifacts and I want to show it to my grandson. If it is off display in the back is there any possibility we might see it, just glimpse it?"

"I'm afraid the moths ate it in the Forties and we threw it out," says the curator who is now staring at his shoes with a distinct air of shame weighing on his shoulder.

Tears seem to well-up in my grandmother's eyes. She reaches into her handbag where she keeps the small hard candies called Tom Thumbs that she always buys in little blue and silver paper bags in Eaton's basement. Her white handkerchief that is scented with Lilly of the Valley emerges. She also hands me a cherry Tom Thumb to take the sting off the shock and wipes her eyes with the handkerchief. There is a long moment of silence.

"How could you? How could you just throw it out?" she says as a cloud of incomprehension wraps her face. The guard and the curator both clear their throats and bow their heads as if they are going to say a prayer. "We are so very sorry," they say in unison, and I expect one of them to pronounce an "Amen." My grandmother is stricken. I can see it in her face. A link to the past has been broken. An important piece of Anglo-Canada has been irretrievably lost.

Determined that the day is not to be lost also, my grandmother announces "Let's go downtown and see if we can find your grandfather in the crowds and meet up with him for lunch at the Georgian Room."

At City Hall, the crowds are thick so we make our way south on Bay Street. The City Hall clock is about to chime. I hold onto my grandmother's hand for fear of being separated in the crush of bodies. People are shouting and hollering and hugging each other as if we had just won a war. My grandmother's spring kid gloves wrap around my hands. I can feel her fingers inside them as we push through the crowds. We head further south on Bay, looking for an opening in the crowd so I can see. We hug the granite and marble and polished brass fronts of the stores.

I am wearing my new birthday outfit — a navy blue blazer that is piped in white. Blue and the white are the colours of my city. I have a small Eton cap that sits almost toward the back of my curly red hair. The front of the cap is emblazoned with crossed flags that represent solidarity, the union of empire and country, the Red Ensign of Canada and the Union Jack of Britain. The wooly grey short pants are chaffing against my legs, and the high knee socks feel tight around my calves. This, I have been told, is the uniform of a school boy and I will be starting kindergarten at the end of the summer. The Eton cap itches my scalp, so I take it off whenever I can because it is hot and makes my head water.

The avenue is echoing, not just because the City Hall clock has boomed the toll of the quarter to noon, but because I hear bagpipe music farther down the street. "Scotland the Brave." "A Hundred Pipers." The snares hiss and the drums boom. This is a moment of pride for everyone. It is the first time I feel pride though I do not know why, the first time that I sense that I am part of something larger. My heart pounds.

My Nana pushes me through the crowds that stand ten to fifteen deep, shoulder to shoulder along the edge of the sidewalk. She calls out "You-hooo! Give the boy a curb." Someone replies in a sarcastic voice that used to mark off a downtown man from an uptowner in old Toronto, "Hey lady, how 'bout we give him a slap in the head?" I am slightly afraid. A hand pushes me from behind and I hear some unknown lady's voice behind my ear saying "Go ahead. You have to witness this."

A man's hand points down to the cement lip where I perch myself. I wrap my arms around my legs and I hunch to rest my chin on my bare white knees. The red brick gutter is beneath my feet that are pinched by my tight black shoes. I am about to witness to history.

The 48th Highlanders, Toronto's Regiment, come marching up Bay Street as if they are drawn to the magnet of the City Hall tower. Pleats of the pipers' kilts sway like stalks of wheat ready for the harvest. Red and white pom-poms on the end of the bass drummer's sticks spin through the air and crescendo in a heartbeat on the skin of the bass drum. The entire street vibrates to the inspiration of the footsteps of the Highlanders' feet in rhythm to their march. The drum major of the band raises his silver mace toward the sky and it catches the glint of sun that has just broken through the clouds, and for an instant I am almost blinded by the light that has caught my eye.

A bass drum beats. The snares roll an introduction. The pipes rev up to a single note and the brass chimes in. They are playing "The Maple Leaf Forever." The crowd on the sidewalk shouts its approval. This is their moment. This is my moment. I want to sing along but I cannot remember the words other than "In days of yore" and "Wolfe the dauntless hero came," and I know that my voice will be drowned out by the sound. I clap wildly.

The band moves forward in their march and behind them are pale blue Cadillac convertibles with their tops down and their chrome glinting, their horns honking, and their headlights flashing on and off and on again. The parade of vehicles stretches down Bay Street as far as the eye can see. People in the office windows above are throwing paper onto the street as if to make a carpet for the cars. On top of the rear seat of each car sit two men in suits who are waving at the cheering crowds.

In the first car, hugged between an older man in a fedora and a younger man with dark eyes and a brush cut is a large trophy, and it too catches the sun, but more so. It almost floats between the two men. It is topped with a large bowl and the man with the brush cut leans over and keeps kissing it between his waves to the gushing approval of the crowd. I have, for the first time in my life, looked upon the Stanley Cup.

The parade's progress stops for a moment. The Highlanders have reached the City Hall. In the second convertible there are two men. One is a square-jawed, brush-cut man whose face looks so very simple beneath its broad, straight eyebrows. The other has red hair and a large, slightly sideways toothy grin. I look up from the curb and I wave my Eton cap above my head and cheer as loudly as I can.

The man with the brush cut and the square jaw looks right at me. He stares directly into my eyes as if he and I are the only ones on the street. He points at me. I point back. He turns and nudges the red-haired man beside him and points me out to him. The two look at me again and the red-haired man stands up, points to his own carrot top which is as bright a red as mine and hollers "High ya red!" as their Cadillac jerks forward and the parade moves again. The two men in the Cadillac are Red Kelly and Tim Horton.

I am part of their Stanley Cup parade. From that moment on, I have writ my name in the blood squeezed from an autumn maple leaf on my grandmother's boulevard. I am sworn to live and die each spring with the fortunes of the blue and white. I am a Maple Leaf forever.

And just as the buds open on the maple trees and throw their arms wide in a celebration of life that is real and alive and infused in everything — the city, the tree-lined streets, the sound of traffic downtown, and the subtle swoosh of wind through the maples I hear at night as I lie in my bed — I am part of all of it. "Toronto," I repeat to myself as I fall asleep in the spare bedroom at my grandparents' house. "I live in Toronto. I am a brother to a baby sister now. This is where I belong."

And when I finally arrive at the temple where the blue and white knights guard their grail, only to see it vanish years later so that it becomes invisible to all except those who keep the faith of the solemn knights of 1962, I stand at the threshold of the Carleton Street entrance of the grandest garden I have ever seen — Maple Leaf Gardens — and the sign in front of me tells me that I reside at the centre of the world, the meridian from which all time and exploration of the world is measured:

←WEST | EAST →

I SAY THE WALLS SHALL CRUMBLE DOWN

And the meek shall inherit the earth
as the skies brighten from a whirlwind
exhaled from forty years of pain.

I have seen the towers bow beneath
the weight of victors and the skies
flood with an uprising of startled birds;

and the blue of heaven dip its hand
into the grey passages of the city
to paint faithful hearts in mightiness.

And I saw the chalice borne aloft,
the glint and its message clear to all.
There shall come a time of joy again.

And I knew the wicked had been cast down
and sun could fill the concourse of a child.
I, from the gutter, looked up and wept.

The procession bled the colour of the sky —
so much blue I thought the seas had parted
and the righteous had been raised up

as someone bannered me beneath the arms.
And I saw the Chief clutch it as he came,
and Imlach beside him in the open car.

There was Kelly. There was Horton. There
was a moment in the silence before all
fell to greater silence no one answered.

And I have suffered in the Ninevehs
of seasons that never seemed to end,
in the parched mouth that yearns to see

them drink again in holy supplication.
O, it shall come again to redeem us all.
I see the shining cup. I still believe in mercy.

FIRST INTERMISSION: SKATING

I looked from the living room window in the early grey light of a December morning and saw my father standing in our garden. New snow had fallen in the night and covered the trees and grass with a smooth, even blanket of decoration. And in that first light I saw his grey-blue shadow and his breath curling in tiny clouds from his mouth. The first rumble and muttering of the city's morning traffic could be heard through the glass. He looked lonely as he stood there with the garden hose in-hand. A trickle of water drizzled onto the snow. A silver drop of liquid sat on the end of his nose like an acrobat balancing over a precipice.

By the time I washed and dressed and made my way into the kitchen where my mother was cooking breakfast, my father had already left for work. I asked her what he was doing in the garden on such a cold morning.

"You're up awfully early," was her only reply. I simply shrugged off the episode as another unexplained eccentricity of my parents' adult lives, another odd ritual or behaviour that in time I would come to understand.

That night, after my father and I had finished my arithmetic homework and the endless columns of long division and carryings of sixes and sevens which left me just that, I heard the back door close quietly, and I made my way again to the living room window. Beneath the starlight, my father's figure seemed to grow against the white snow. His shadow was cast in a deep navy blue by the glow from the kitchen window. His thumb pressed against the nozzle and the spray caught in the wind flew back in his face covering his toque with a myriad of tiny stars that glistened in an icy constellation. I grew tired and went to bed.

This ritual kept up for several more mornings and nights. "Dad is building a rink in the garden, isn't he," I said matter-of-factly to my mother after the third morning of spraying. "Does this mean I can learn to skate?"

"Your father is quite the skater himself," she replied. "Before I met him, he cut quite a figure on the blades. When we were courting he'd take me down to Grenadier Pond and we'd skate round and round beneath the moon to the most beautiful music you ever heard. There's nothing like the cold wind in your face and the feel of speed as your edges cut into the ice. If you ask him nicely during the holidays, he'll teach you how."

When I woke or just before I went to bed, my father would be out in the garden hosing down the backyard in the silence of the winter stillness. The yard grew slick with the sheet of ice that gradually hardened into a greyish-white slab that shone as smooth as a mirror.

On the morning after a heavy snowfall, I heard the scraping of a shovel and watched him piling banks of drift at the edge of the rink. I realized it was the first morning of the holidays and I went back to bed to dream of skating.

I dreamed that I was the fastest skater in the world and that the entire Toronto Maple Leaf team appeared over the rim of our garden fence to ask me to skate for them in the final game of the playoffs. I had seen the games on television when the Saturday night babysitters let me stay up that late. The players moved over the white surface of the ice like beautiful swift eagles through a clear blue sky, gracefully swooping in on goal and lifting their sticks in triumph. I longed to skate like those players, like jets, like hawks, like lightning.

That morning, after I had washed and dressed and eaten breakfast to my mother's satisfaction, I went outside to the garden and stood before the rink. The sun had just broken through the tarnished clouds that arched over the city, and the small halo of yellow light around the glow filled the garden with a delicate splendour. The ice spread from fence to fence in a silver carpet, and I stepped aboard the surface and carefully slid across it in my boots. For an instant I was at Maple Leaf Gardens and the crowd was chanting my name.

Christmas morning started early at our house. As the first light crept over the backyard fence, I tip-toed bleary-eyed into the living room and stood in front of the tree. Beneath the spreading green boughs and red and silver ornaments was large box in candy-cane paper with a bow on top and my name on the card.

"Go ahead and open it," my father said as he stood quietly in the doorway and tied the sashes of his bathrobe. My mother followed him into the room and sat down on the couch. I tore at the paper. The blue and black and red cardboard box beneath shone with the words "Bauer Deluxe

Figures. Boys Size." Figures! Figure skates? The Leafs didn't wear figure skates. My face fell.

"Now you can learn to skate like your Dad," my mother said proudly. I could tell that my father had seen the look of utter defeat on my face during the instant that the true nature of the blades registered in my mind.

After the Queen's message and the official greetings from members of the government, my father took me out to the garden, sat me down at the picnic table, and helped me into the new skates. He crouched and tugged as the laces fed first through the eyelets and then through the rows of black metal tongues that gripped and tightened above my ankles. Then he bent over and put on his own skates. I stood and my ankles bent beneath me.

"Mine are made of kangaroo leather to help me jump better. They don't make them like that anymore," he announced proudly, the words clouding from his lips with every vowel. His boots were soft and supple whereas mine were stiff and bit like clamps into my lower shins.

He stepped over the banked snow and literally sailed across the garden. I stepped over the mounded edge and landed on my face. My feet suddenly felt very strange. They refused to hold me up no matter how hard I tried to balance on the thin strips of metal that glimmered beneath me.

My father floated over and grabbed me under the arms and pulled me up. "A couple of times around just to get your balance and soon you'll be flying." He held me up like a rag doll as my blades and feet dragged along beneath me. Within an hour I had managed to stand upright in my own painful little evolution. I took an uneasy step forward and started to move. I think I was skating.

"Let's see you do your edges," my father called from the other side of the garden. "Get the edge and it will be easy." He demonstrated by turning effortlessly in a neat circle like a falcon hovering in a summer sky.

Edges? Every time I leaned even the slightest bit sideways, over I went. My arms and legs were covered in white. My rear was becoming damp and cold. The legs of my pants stiffened and turned solid. When I did manage to move forward I often caught my picks and went face first onto the ice. The situation was soon hopeless. My thoughts of becoming a Maple Leaf rapidly dimmed before my eyes.

As my mother set the Christmas turkey before us with all the pomp and ceremony we accorded the bird in our house, and as my father gripped the carving knife and drew it several times against the sharpener, my mother asked how the skating was going. How on earth could I tell her that I was terrible? "Always try to do your best," she would tell me. A terrible feeling of disappointment welled up from my stomach. Over dinner I thought I could gradually approach the core of the problem.

"I'm not sure I'm made for figure skates," abruptly came out, although that wasn't quite the way I had meant to say it. My parents looked at each other silently. I hadn't really meant to say it that way. I wanted to say that I would keep trying, that I would be a great figure skater like my father, but at that age one of the problems with life is that statements seldom leave the mouth as they are intended. "I really want to be a hockey player. Like the Maple Leaf guys on TV." My father simply smiled at my mother and asked me if I wanted more turkey.

The next day I did not take to the rink. The skates sat in the corner of my room with their tongues hanging out, taunting me. By the middle of the week, they had become part of the landscape of my own little space, hardly noticeable amid the jetsam of clothes and toys. One morning I discovered they were gone.

"Where are the skates?" I asked my mother.

She shrugged. "You didn't seem to be cut out for them. I guess your father has taken them back to the store." I felt awful. I realized just how much my father had wanted me to be a figure skater. "Keep trying, you'll find your edge," I heard him saying in my mind over and over again. I stared out the living room window at the rink. It lay grey and dejected beneath the overcast sky. A soft wind blew a tiny snow devil across its emptiness.

But when my father came home from work that night, tired after a long day caused by the time off for Christmas, he carried under his arm a cardboard box, without any wrapping except for a simple paper bag. This time a black and white box read "Bauer Hockey Skates — Boys Size."

I immediately laced them on all by myself and wobbled out the backdoor to the garden with my hockey stick and a puck. My rubbery little ankles splayed sideways, and I grunted and strained to move forward with no more grace of motion than a landslide. But I was, at last, a hockey player and I chased the puck around the rink until my mother called me into bed. As I took off the boots, the burning sensation of blisters shot through my feet, but I didn't care. The Maple Leafs would find me yet.

The years have passed. I have suffered and suffered again with my favourite team. I keep dreaming that they will find me. I also dream of a winter night long ago when I saw my own life spread before me. Although I did not know it at the time, it was a foreshadowing of my own chosen path of painful grinding because I did not have the patience or perhaps the foresight to follow the ways and dreams my parents laid before me in their gifts of love and caring. Doing things the hard way has become my way of life. And my parents? I realize that all they ever wanted for me was to be happy.

And in the small hours of that night when my father came home with the hockey skates, I thought I was dreaming when I woke to the sound of the shovel gently moving across the rink in our backyard. I rose from my bed and tip-toed silently downstairs to the living room window where I parted the curtains and peered into the moonlit shadows that hovered about our house.

In the blue and somber tones of the snowy midnight vista, I saw the outline of my father gliding quietly around the garden, easing effortlessly from one foot to the other. His body was graceful and streamlined, soaring elegantly among the stars that reached down to lift him up into their splendour, his silver blades passing through the solid surface of the ice and trailing immaculate thin lines behind him like a draftsman crafting a beautiful and intricate design. He mohawked and danced with his arms extended from his body and leapt almost weightlessly into the cold and silent air.

"Keep trying," I hear him saying still in my mind as if it was only seconds ago. "Keep trying and you'll find your edge."

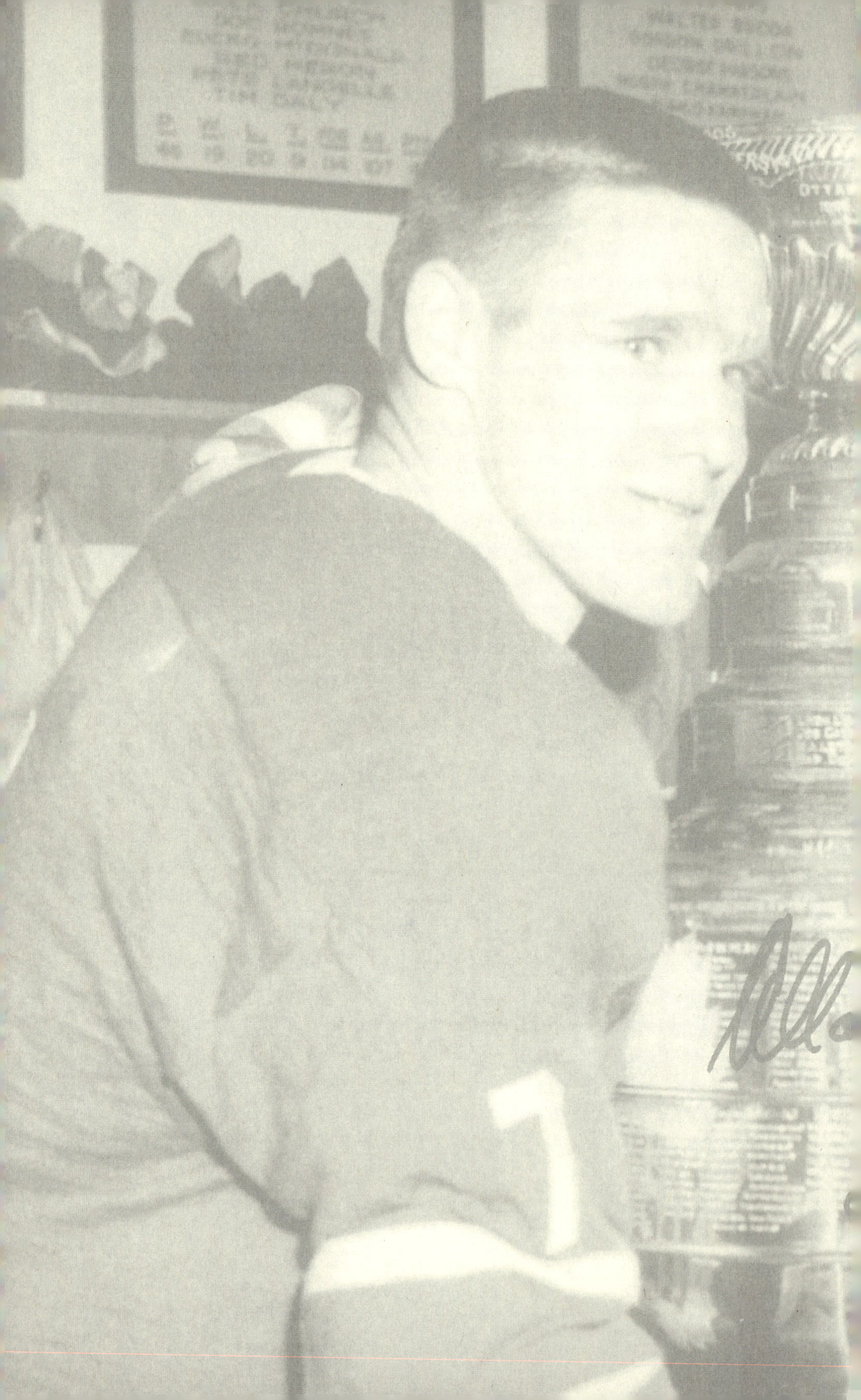

SECOND PERIOD

THE BUDS ON MY GRANDPARENTS' MAPLE TREE

The Maple Leaf

There is a powerful spirit of mysticism inherent in sports. Rational people will deny it, but it is there. The dark legends of defeat and the bright icons of victory are part of every game. Why do Detroit fans throw octopi on the ice during the playoffs? Why have the Chicago Cubs never won a World Series since they dismissed their manager Muldoon in the 1930s or since they tossed out the man with the goat during the 1908 intra-league final? For every rational statistic, every super-analyzed play or money ball or money hockey solution to an equation, there is a folk belief hiding in the background that explains why a team's fortunes are as they are.

I am no exception. I love the statistics but I want answers that are not to be found in the realm of rational thought. I want to bring my imagination to the game and the game to my imagination. And when defeat keeps repeating and repeating itself, one must question if some strange, unearthly force is at work to thwart the aspirations of fans who crave victory more than anything else.

As a Toronto Maple Leafs fan, I have waited since 1967 to see a particular game end and a cup hoisted over the heads of Toronto players. I am waiting for that "next year" that never seems to arrive though I do believe it will arrive…someday…whenever. And I have asked myself why my team has to dwell so long in such futility. Losing seasons to a sports fan is the equivalent of the Babylonian captivity to an ancient Israelite. "How long, O Lord, how long?" What nemesis, either external or internal, is the cause for such misery? Why does my team always seem to be on the road to Thebes on a bright sunny day when suddenly something dark leaps into its path to set in motion a whole series of unfortunate events that lead to downfall?

Einstein says that repeating the same action over and over again and expecting different results is a form of insanity. So be it. But, as Carl Jung suggested, insanity is also the next door neighbour of the mythic mind. Myth is a way of explaining the world to ourselves when we do not have the beauty and rationality of science to make sense of what we see. We turn to the imagination and the imagination looks for causes for an event. My team has been losing. Why? Here, for what it is worth and for the best of intentions, is my theory.

Hockey crests: in particular, the maple leaf on the front of every jersey is to blame. Our emblem dear. Our emblem tinkered with. Hockey team logos say a great deal about the team. They are meant to be symbols of the traditions and the ideas that the team wishes to instill in its fans. For some team logos, there is an implied history and a tradition that is communicated by the image on the front of the jersey. In some cases, the great teams of sports have had the same logo, the same team crest, for almost a century. Think of the New York Yankees' crest and you will see the shadows of Babe Ruth and Joe DiMaggio lurking in the corner of the N or the Y. Think of the Montreal Canadiens and the ghosts of Rocket Richard and Jean Beliveau emerge carrying a torch to pass to the next generation of players. A team crest for both fans and players carries a lot of weight, sometimes so much so that it is hard for the players that don the jersey to live up to their team's history under the pressure and scrutiny of fans. From the perspective of the fans, the team crest is part legend, part myth, part chronicle, and, at times, a religious icon in the passionate belief in sports that fans embrace. The sons of many of my friends have their bedrooms painted in Maple Leafs blue with Maple Leafs curtains and bed spreads and even garbage cans. That is iconography at its finest.

The original six NHL team crests are wonders of longevity in marketing. A number of cultural theorists have suggested that there is something mesmerizing and hypnotic about the Montreal Canadiens' horseshoe C with the H in the middle of it. In the case of the Boston Bruins' B in the centre of a wheel, one can see something almost Hindu in the idea of a hub with spokes radiating from the centre. The B seems to float to the left, as if it is about to deke the beholder. The winged wheel of Detroit suggests motion, flight, and swiftness. The Chicago crest has come under scrutiny in recent times for its appropriation of indigenous identity, though many players still claim that Chicago's is their favourite uniform. Even the New York Rangers, with the writing that seems to tumble from the sky as if paper in a ticker-tape parade carries a sense of beauty and simplicity. The only crest that has changed and struggled to evolve over the century of NHL play is that of the Toronto Maple Leafs.

The Leafs' crest contains a spelling mistake. The plural of leaf is leaves. The team should be The Toronto Maple Leaves. The original intention was that each player was a leaf, a vital extension of a kind of *arbor vita* or tree of life. The tree has stood on the University of Toronto's crest for almost two hundred years in honour of the university's motto: *velut arbor aevo* or like a tree may it grow. To stroll through the districts of the city of Toronto is to walk beneath and honour guard of branches that meet over the streets, or to be reminded that the arch of maple branches over the avenues is like the vaulted ceilings of the great English cathedrals. The city has always had a profound connection with trees. Toronto has been called "the Forest City," though that title officially belongs to London, Ontario. Throughout the city a person is reminded of the tree of life. When the Toronto hockey club began as the Blue and White, the old orchards still stood in the north end, and the valleys of the Don and Humber rivers were gardens of maple trees. It is little wonder that Toronto's NHL team has what Northrop Frye called "a vegetative device" as its symbol. Trees are symbols of growth where what is small will eventually become mighty.

From a purely botanical perspective, the leaf of the *acer saccharum* or sugar maple has, on average, nineteen points whereas the maple leaf on the front of the Toronto hockey club's jersey has had a varying number of points during its history. As a result of this comparison between the organic maple leaf and the logo of the hockey team, it is possible to suggest that the fortunes of the hockey club are linked to the number of points of the leaf on the team's logo.

When Conn Smythe bought the struggling Toronto St. Pats franchise in 1926 (formerly the Toronto Arenas, formerly the Toronto Blue and Whites), the Colonel, as he was known from his wartime service in the Canadian Corps, changed the name to the Maple Leafs. He did away with the bright green jerseys of the St. Pats. Green would not be the official colour of an NHL franchise again until the Minnesota North Stars joined the league during the first expansion in 1968. Smythe went with Toronto's traditional civic colours, the blue and white of the University of Toronto where he had studied prior to the war, when he crafted the identity that became the Toronto Maple Leafs. In an oddity of history, the Maple Leafs were the last of the original six teams to assert their colours and logos on the hockey world. When the blue and white leaf arrived, Boston, New York, Chicago and Detroit had already become part of the nascent NHL.

The Maple Leaf on the front of the jersey, as Smythe pictured it, was a tribute to the men he had served with in the war who had given their lives for their country, or as the second verse of Muir's anthem puts it, "For freedom, home, and loved ones dear firmly stood and nobly died." During World War One, Canadian regiments had been told to dispense with their local regimental badges and to don one uniform cap brass: the maple leaf. The leaf was in tribute not only to Muir's anthem but to the fact that the maple was the one tree that grew in all ten provinces. It was a symbol of unity for the troops, a badge of the blood sacrifice that Canadians had made at Vimy and Passchendaele, and Smythe knew just how powerful such a symbol could be to a nation that had come of age in the trenches of France and Belgium. The generation that watched the blue and white had known, perhaps too well, the devastation of their era's Lundy's Lane.

The Montreal Canadiens, in an attempt to keep up with the sense of national blood sacrifice that identified the Maple Leafs, eventually painted a few lines from John McCrae's rondeau that currently graces the back of the Canadian paper ten dollar bill: "Take up our quarrel with the foe / To you with failing hands we throw / The torch, be yours to hold it high." The Maple Leafs did not protest. After all, McCrae had taught at McGill University, though his name as a victim of the war is inscribed on the Soldier's Tower Memorial at the University of Toronto along with the names of fallen classmates of Conn Smythe.

What Smythe did not realize was that though his team was The Toronto Maple Leafs Hockey Club, and each player on that club was "a Leaf," the team name would go down in history as one of the most accepted spelling mistakes. Perhaps he thought that a team is made of the collective effort of individuals, and that each Leaf had something to contribute toward the greater success. Spelling is always the first casualty in sports.

The original maple leaf that Smythe chose to be the emblem of his hockey club in 1926 had thirty-four points. The symmetry of the leaf is slightly askance and it appears to be twisting in the wind. Through the years, the number of points on the leaf decreased as the leaf became more stylized.

When the Leafs won the Stanley Cup in 1962, their emblem actually increased the number of points to thirty-five, but by the time the team won its last championship in 1967 the number had shrunken to eleven. A year later when Harold Ballard took over the team, he reduced the leaf on the logo to a ten point device, perhaps to honour the nation's ten provinces; after all, Leaf broadcasts on the CBC until 1967 always opened with Foster Hewitt's famous call, "Hello hockey fans in Canada and the United States." The Leafs were once Canada's team if not hockey's team, the icons of the English half of the nation, and spokespersons for a mythology and culture that has lost consciousness of itself in the way that the team emblem lost twenty points or more.

What is hard for many Maple Leafs fans to swallow…the constant reminder of lost glory…is the almost fifty year absence of a Stanley Cup victory. That absence may be interpreted by some believers in sympathetic magic (something that is rife in the mythology of sports) as the sign that the magical power of the team's symbol is waning. When the extra points were returned to the Maple Leaf crest as a third jersey gesture in recent years, the fortunes of the team have perked up, though only momentarily.

As a ten-year-old fan who saw the first period of Game Six in 1967, I begged the Maple Leafs to bring back the missing points on their leaf logo. I also begged to stay up and see the game to its conclusion. I was denied. Instead, I saw the image pruned, and the last thing I remember from that night in April of Canada's centennial year was my mother saying "Time for bed. You can stay up and watch them win the cup next year." Next year has never come.

Our Emblem Dear

When my grandfather lay on his deathbed in 1974, I sat with him through the long, hot summer afternoons in his North Toronto home that for all its beauty and sturdy oak woodwork was not air conditioned. Between bouts of pain, he would tell me stories, all of which concluded with a maxim. He told me how he had been late getting home one evening around 1900 because he had gone to see Sir Wilfrid Laurier speak at a hall in the downtown. He dared not tell his father what he had done. His father was a strict Tory.

Laurier had so impressed my grandfather that he made me promise that I would always vote Liberal. I asked him why. "They have a vision of a future I won't live to see but you will," he replied, and closed his eyes. Toronto was, for many years, a Liberal stronghold. I arrived at my grandparents' house one day, around the time the Leafs won their first cup of the Sixties, and found Lester Pearson sipping lemonade on the front porch with my grandfather. Mitchell Sharp was with them. Sharp went to our church and always greeted me as "young future Liberal." The vision of the future, from whatever Laurier said that evening at the turn of the century when my grandfather was little more than a teenager must have matched the spirit of the city in my grandfather's dreams.

My grandfather also made me promise one other thing, and that was easy to agree to: I would never stop cheering for the Leafs. The blue and white ran in my veins from the day that Horton looked me in the eye on Bay Street. I asked my grandfather what had been the moment that brought him to the Church of Church and Carleton. There was a long moment of silence. His eyes were closed. I thought it was the pain sinking its dagger into his stomach. But when he opened his eyes I knew he had been somewhere else in his dreams.

The Maple Leaf Forever

My grandfather was born in 1885 and grew up in a family of eight children in a small house at 321 Carleton Street, a dead-end avenue that runs from the lip of the Don Valley to the world's longest avenue, Yonge Street. At Yonge, Carleton becomes the serious College Street. Carleton Street is named for the British General Sir Guy Carleton. It was Carleton who, as the Governor of Lower Canada (Quebec) told French Canada it could keep its language and its religion after Quebec had been exchanged in the Treaty of Paris for the sugar island of Guadalupe.

In my grandfather's youth, Carleton Street began in an area that later became known as Cabbagetown, though in his childhood the terminus of Carleton Street was a residential area, a mixture of prosperity and working middle class people whose Victorian homes were old even by Toronto standards of the time. 321 Carleton is almost at the end of the street where the Necropolis, Toronto's city of the dead, meets the city of living. The house was part of a row of workers' homes. Many of those workers spent their days toiling in the factories that had become integrated into the neighbourhood.

Beneath the end of Carleton Street where the hillside of the city slanted down to the Don was a large flatland beside the river. In the winter, especially after heavy autumn rains overflowed the banks, the Don flats would freeze and form a natural rink. The children who lived on the heights above looked after the rink because it was their communal property, shovelling it off after snowfalls and patching gouges with ice melted by the warmth of their hands. And because the rink also lay in the shadow of the Necropolis, death always hovered over their impromptu games of shinny and their moments of childhood glory.

To keep their skates warm during the hike down the hillside to the rink, they would have their mothers cook baked potatoes and stuff the hot spuds in the toes of their skates. The potatoes would reside inside their boots as they skated. When it came time to return home, they were fortified on the trek back up the slippery slope by having the potato for a snack. In the summer, when the flats dried out, the space reverted to a field for what was then Canada's national sport, and became the best lacrosse ground in the city; and unlike the more pristine rinks and lacrosse grounds closer to the city's core, no one was ever turned away and told they couldn't join the play. Winter hockey was the everyman sport.

My grandfather's idol was his older brother, a very brilliant, handsome lad named Jim. Unlike my grandfather who was frail all his life though fast on his skates and on his legs, Jim who was five years older than my grandfather was a natural athlete, tall, big-boned and strong. Hockey came to him like breathing. There was something electric about his charm and personality, and he was gifted with a love of science. At the age of sixteen Jim became an apprentice electrician but died of an appendectomy while the family holidayed in a tent on Toronto Island.

The household needed another salary to replace the meager, lost wage that Jim had brought in. My grandfather put away his school books, his skates, and his winter afternoons on the flats, and went to work as a delivery boy for a dry goods firm at Front and Wellington, named for its owner, Senator John McDonald. For the next six years, working for a dollar a week, he rode a penny-farthing bicycle through the streets of Toronto and earned a reputation as an honest, caring worker. Following the death of a higher up on the *Lusitania* during World War One and having served his employer faithfully and honestly by making the trip to England himself, my grandfather rose to become chief buyer for the firm. It was a well-salaried job for the time, and he was able to pay for what his family needed, put some money away for the future, and spend a little on what he loved. And what did he do with his pay cheque after his family had been fed and housed and clothed? Life could take the boy out of hockey, but it could not take the hockey out of the boy. He bought season tickets to watch the Toronto Blueshirts, the Blue and Whites, at the Mutual Street Arena.

When he married my grandmother in 1921, he brought her into the fraternity of hockey society in Toronto. Their honeymoon was spent at a resort north of Toronto, a place called Woodington that is now a golf course in the Muskokas. Hand in hand they strolled along the tree lined pathways. They purchased a small painting from the gift shop, a water-colour of the trail where they had wandered idyllically. The honeymoon seemed to be going fine until they sat down at their table in the dining room midway through the week.

My grandfather stood up. "That's Harry Watson over there!" Harry Watson played for the Toronto Granites, a competing team that played out of prestigious curling club and that had won the Memorial Cup a few years before on a challenge. Harry Watson was their leading scorer. My grandfather sauntered over to Watson's table and struck up a conversation. The next morning my grandfather was up well before dawn. Bleary-eyed, my grandmother asked what he was doing.

"Harry and I are going fishing."

For the next several days, my grandfather and Harry Watson were inseparable. They presented themselves as best buddies. My grandmother sat on the porch of the resort and read a magazine, then a book of poems, then a novel. On the last night of the week, Harry came up to their table with a "mind if I join you two old married folks?"

"We're not old and we haven't been married long," my grandmother scowled. "This is our honeymoon." All apologies, Harry withdrew under my grandfather's protests.

"Ida, why did you do that? Don't you know he's a hockey player?" Though the latter part of the week and the way my grandfather spent it hurt my grandmother, love did conquer all, especially hockey.

Each game night my grandparents would meet downtown which was a considerable distance from their tiny first house on Woodbine Avenue. They would sit on the bench seating in the lower section of the Mutual Street building and cheer for the Toronto Arenas (the team had changed its name) in their blue and white uniforms. One game, my grandfather became so excited as he tried to follow the play into the far end of the rink that he accidently knocked my grandmother off the end bench. She tumbled down a flight of steps. The ushers came running.

"Hey, what are you doing?" They shouted at him as they tried to pick my grandmother up off the concrete.

"Did you see that?" he asked them. "That was crooked. He pulled that man down on a break-away." The ushers forgave him, but the hurt of hockey never really left my grandmother. At the age of seven when I was playing right wing in our church league — I was nothing more than an ice duster balancing badly on bandy legs — I told my grandmother I wanted to grow up to be a hockey player. "Absolutely not," she said. "You will break all your teeth." That was the end of that conversation.

The last straw for my grandmother and hockey came one evening on a very rainy November night. The streetcars had stopped running and the city was in darkness. My grandparents began their walk from Woodbine down to the Mutual Street Arena. Soaked and shivering from the five mile hike, an attendant at the door told them that the game had been cancelled because there was no electricity in the city. "That's awful!" said my grandfather. "Harry Watson was playing for the visitors tonight!"

God Save Our King

The trade off for the demise of the seasons tickets was a new home in the north end and a large radio that my grandfather could turn up loud to listen to the games. He had been deaf since childhood and his enthusiasm for a play, he told me, was read in the faces of other fans when the cheering drowned out the play by play. By the end of the decade as the Stock Market crashed and my grandparents struggled to make ends meet, the hero of the hometown crew was King Clancy. My grandfather would take up his leaning stance each game night in his large arm chair. Running his hands through his hair and squeezing the upholstered arm caps as Foster Hewitt described a tense moment, the chair soon needed reupholstering. The Gardens opened despite the hard times. The Leafs had been born and had the grandest home of any NHL team.

When the crash came in October of 1929, my grandfather had lost most of his money. John McDonald, the owner of the dry goods firm, passed away suddenly leaving my grandfather without a job. My mother had been born as well. Points disappeared from the maple leaf on the players' jerseys so that the fifty of the Charlie Conacher and Joe Primeau (1927 to 1934) vintage were reduced to thirty-nine (1935 to 1937). The disappearance of the extra points had an impact on the Leafs. During that time they did not win a Stanley Cup.

Conn Smythe must have sensed that his team's fortunes were flagging. There had not been a cup win in a decade. In 1938 he redesigned the maple leaf on the jersey. The new leaf showed signs of maturity with veins appearing in the logo's background; but it also depicted a symmetry of thirty-four points. That logo would remain on the front of every Toronto Maple Leaf player for the next twenty years. During that twenty year period, the Leafs emerged as one of the dominant franchises in the NHL winning six cups, including five cups in a row between 1945 and 1949. Then the drought came again.

Hockey success runs in cycles. Few teams, with the exception of the preternatural Montreal Canadiens, are continually successful. The Cup drought from 1951 to 1962 was a reminder that fortune is cyclical, that the good must come with the bad. No one, however, could have anticipated the drought that would start for the Toronto Maple Leafs in 1967. The impact of the 1967 championship, the two Canadian teams — English Canada versus French Canada, hatless Wolfe against Montcalm — was such that Toronto's last victory became ingrained on the city's consciousness to the point that the moment had to be relived and revisited. The final game airs at least twice a month on the Leafs' cable television channel. There is always the sense one has at the end of each replay of that game that something went terribly wrong right after that. Expansion? Bad trades? Dark scandals in the underbelly of the Gardens? Absurd ownership? No one has figured it out. The game continues to be replayed as if it was the last clear thought in someone's brain.

When the College Street subway station platforms were remodelled in the late Seventies, the TTC commissioned artist Charles Pachter (he of the Queen mounted on a moose while trooping the colours) to immortalize the eternal struggle of the Maple Leafs and the Canadiens on a series of enameled murals. The Leafs appear on the southbound platform (and the message in that became a self-fulfilling prophecy of doom as the team's fortunes literally headed south and the franchise lost some of its lustre from the Conn Smythe days) and the Canadiens on the northbound platform (and the Habs presence became metaphorically linked not only to the top of the standings but to the Canadian identity of a northern giant).

The owner of the Maple Leafs, Harold Ballard, was so incensed that Pachter would portray the Montreal team on the platform for the stop for the Gardens that he got a court order that forbid Pachter from putting the words "Toronto Maple Leafs" on the front of the now ten point leaf on the Toronto jerseys. The shadows of Toronto players such as Rick Vaive, and goaltenders Mike Palmateer and Paul Harrison from the Seventies remain forever with ellipses on their chests. The Canadiens on the other platform — the ghosts of Guy Lafleur, Steve Shutt, and Ken Dryden — bear their eternal C with the H in the middle of it. Their logo is as fresh as the day it was invented. In the eyes of Torontonians, they are the spiritual winners of the 1967 Cup. No one has obliterated their mythology.

Toronto, under Ballard, defeated itself. The Ballard years were the dark years for most Toronto fans. There were child abuse scandals at the Gardens. There were seasons when nothing went right. Finishing last one year garnered Toronto the remarkable talents of Wendel Clark who was eventually traded for the even more epic figure of Mats Sundin. Neither ever won a cup as a Maple Leaf. When the time came for a new corporate vision of the Leafs to emerge post-Ballard, a vision that somehow matched the city around the game, a city that had evolved from faces on the street to faces in the boardroom, the move to the new Air Canada Centre signaled something remarkable: the return of the multi-pointed Maple Leaf as a third jersey concept. Perhaps the past was not lost after all. Perhaps the magic will return. I wait.

And Heaven Bless

The Christmas of my sixth year, I announced to my parents and grandparents that I wanted to play hockey, and in particular wanted to play hockey for the Toronto Maple Leafs. Under the tree that year (1963) I found a hockey stick, a pair of blue and white gloves (oversized) with the multi-pointed Maple Leaf logo on them, and a wool hockey sweater in an Eaton's box.

A sweater just like mine (which I still have) has entered our national consciousness through a story by Quebec writer Roch Carrier, "The Hockey Sweater." The story tells of a boy who desperately wants a Montreal Canadiens wool jersey. The boy's mother writes away to Eaton's mail order department. In what stands as one of cruelest mistakes wrought on a character by a mail order company, the boy receives a Toronto Maple Leafs jersey. He cannot be the hero of his dreams, Maurice 'Rocket' Richard, because his mother refuses to return the sweater to Eaton's in exchange for the correct *bleu, blanc, et rouge* jersey of *Les Habitants*. A passage from the short story adorned the back of the paper version of Canada's five dollar bill until an avid hockey fan, a Prime Minister no less, had it replaced on the plastic currency.

Unlike Roch Carrier's character in his short story "The Hockey Sweater," Eaton's and my mother got it right. After all, my mother had been a devotee of Ted Kennedy who captained the Leafs during their five cups of the 1940s. She, too, knew the mythology of the blue and white from her regular visits to the Junior Marlies games to her passion for all good things Toronto. The blue sweater had the white piping, the laces at the collar, and the logo worn by the 1962 Leafs.

When I skated on the rink in our back garden and fell down, the sweater got wet and gave off a metallic smell — the smell of wet wool that I still associate with the game. When I went to hockey school with some of the neighbourhood boys, I remember that smell of wet wool. Their breaths gave off the reek of stale milk, and the leather of our gloves and pads, soaked from perspiration and ice dust, carried the tang of slaughtered animals whose hides were not quite cured.

When I put on that sweater, I thought I was a champion. I thought I was Frank Mahovlich. I outgrew the sweater in several years. By the time I was twelve it would not go over my head. That is when I broke my back in a school accident. The boy who did it to me ended up on the Olympic ski team and fell just when it looked as if he might win the race. I could not even enjoy victory vicariously through his achievements. I lay on my back for almost a year and then spent three years in a back brace. I still suffer the pain from that injury. The only positive that came out of the back injury was that while I had to give up my dream of being a hockey player and a Toronto Maple Leaf, I read poetry and immersed myself in the knowledge that there was something in every line and verse that was mine forever. Those tedious months on my back are when my career in literature began. Poetry was the safe place where my imagination, my dreams, could not be taken from me. I also became a statistics fanatic. Every year when *Hockey Annual* appeared, I was there in the drug store as it was loaded onto the shelf. Hockey, for me, became something that lived in my imagination. It lived next to poetry. With my ear pressed to an old, plastic GE radio that grew red hot in my head-board, I would listen late into the night to Foster Hewitt calling the road games from the west.

Dreams die hard. What we want in life is not the measure of who we are but of who we imagine ourselves to be. Every time I put on my Leafs jersey, especially my Tim Horton jersey with the 1967 crest, I am for that moment one of my heroes. It feels good. Most of the time life wants to run us down. Donning the colours to watch a game, even if the Leafs lose, is a good thing. Life keeps saying that we cannot live most of our dreams, but nonetheless we dream them anyways and hope for the best.

What hurt most when I was twelve were not the vertebrae or the discs or the muscles that wove themselves into excruciating knots, but that I could not lead the Leafs to victory in some future sudden death seventh game like Bill Barilko.

For every Leafs fan, Barilko is the mythological Arthur who might someday return to lead us to greatness again. He scored the sudden death cup-winning goal in 1951 and then mysteriously vanished into the great wilds of Northern Ontario while on a fishing trip a few weeks later. In some ways, the tragedy for Leafs fans was not merely Barilko's death in 1951, but the discovery of his yellow Fairchild bush plane and his remains in 1962, shortly after the parade that I witnessed. For eleven years, he had been swallowed by Canada while broadcast signals and hockey games and the voice of Leafs play-by-play man Foster Hewitt floated through the air around him. Barilko is the ghost of hope to Leafs fans. He was our King Arthur who, as in the prophecies for the survival of England in its darkest hour, would return and lead our team to victory. His disappearance and his legendary goal are celebrated in the song "Fifty Mission Cap" by the Tragically Hip. That song, like "The Maple Leaf Forever," is embedded in the team's mythology as an anthem of identity for everyone who cheers for the Leafs and dreams of being counted among their ranks.

One day when I was working on my Masters degree at the University of Toronto, I found myself on the way to an appointment around Carleton and Church Street. Out of Maple Leaf Gardens came Pat Boutette, a serviceable and steady checking winger for the Leafs. My aunt had been to his wedding. As we walked past each other I realized, "geez, I am the same size as Pat Boutette. I could have played for the Leafs!" Fans dream. That's their job. They dream not only of seeing the parade to celebrate that victory wind through the streets of their city but of being the one responsible for the victory.

In those imaginative moments between games, fans project themselves into the play and tell themselves that they could have hit that empty net, they could have cleared that puck sitting temptingly on the goal line. Sigmund Freud notes in his essay on the hero that a hero (in this case a particular player or a team of players) is our surrogate in the imaginative action of a work of fiction. Fiction and games are not that far apart. A hockey game is a refereed version of an alternate reality. You can punch someone in a game of hockey and get a two minute penalty. You can punch someone on a street and go to jail for several months. Hockey flirts with the idea that it is not reality. Fiction flirts with the idea that it is reality. Somewhere the two realities rub shoulders. That's where heroes enter into the picture. A player who scores a goal is the protagonist of the moment. As our surrogate, the hero's fortunes become our fortunes. As our representative in the action, his success is our success and his survival is our survival.

Imaginatively, each fan is a player. There is no objectivity in sports, at least from the metaphorical/imaginative perspective. Fans wear the jerseys of their favourite players. My Tim Horton jersey has his famous number seven on the back. That not insane or absurd: that is merely an expression of the desire to feel the joy of victory and the reassurance that survival to fight another day is guaranteed. And in terms of hero worship, he did look me in the eye that day in 1962. And what sits ticking at the core of each fan is a little perpetual motion machine of vicarious anticipation and competition. Having tasted victory once, even if the victory was long ago, the player in the fan wants to taste victory again.

That last hurrah of success in 1967 is set against almost fifty years of futility. I am one of the few lucky ones who was able to witness a bit of that last portion of success as it happened. At the time, it seemed to everyone that the Stanley Cup would take up permanent residence in Toronto. In literal terms, it did. The Cup resides at the Hockey Hall of Fame at the corner of Yonge and Front. Every time I pass by the heavy oak and bronze doors of the old bank building (and the irony that the building was originally the Bank of Montreal is never lost on me) I know that the cup is just a matter of metres from me in the physical world; but in the mythic world of play and imagination (the same place in our minds where literature resides), it is an elusive grail that Toronto fans seek but may never reach. Certainly, we may quest after it and even see the possibilities of it within our grasp, but like Sir Lancelot of the Arthurian legends, it is always too far away to be attained. For me, this is the point at which literature and hockey start to share identities.

When prolonged periods without a championship happen to a sports franchise, fans are willing to look at any cause except reason. These are the moments during which the Classical concept of fate enters the mind. There is a nemesis, some dark force in the universe that is out to defeat the hero or heroes. The defeated, sunken shoulders of the favourite warriors in armour shuffling off the ice as the visitor or outsider team triumphs leaves a fan searching for an answer. Why not us? When will our time come? Who or what is to blame? Where can we find our saviour who will lead us out of the desert? Who will be the star centre we desperately need? What price a miracle?

In Montreal, the Habs fans declare that it is a tragedy if the team does not win the cup. Victory is an expectation. If the Canadiens fail to make the playoffs, the earth has gone out of orbit and the seas have dried up. Is there still a God, they ask? On the walls of the Maple Leafs' dressing room, Conn Smythe did not quote a poem such as "In Flanders Fields" or even a pithy aphorism from Shakespeare or a great statesman. He wrote "Defeat Does Not Rest Lightly On Their Shoulders." That is not to say that Toronto players need to win. It merely states that not winning is something to be absorbed philosophically and understood personally. In this sense, a philosophical reaction to loss is what one finds in Classical tragedy. The hero falls. He looks at his predicament, and explains to himself and his audience why the world around fell apart.

When Randy Carlyle became coach of the Toronto Maple Leafs on March 2, 2012, he changed the statement on the dressing room wall. The wall now reads "Burn all the boats." Carlyle, in his understated yet enlightened way, has refused to explain the quote. It is from Virgil's *Aeneid*. It is from the scene where the Trojan women refuse to continue to look for something elusive and beyond reach, the "ever-retreating horizon" that their leader Aeneas pursues in order to found a new Troy. The women declare that they will look no further for the answer to their dreams. The answer will happen here or nowhere. The answer is within them. The answer is who they are and what has made them. And with that knowledge that they must make a stand, a stand similar to that at Queenston Heights or Lundy's Lane, they burn all the boats.

THE MAPLE LEAF FOREVER

The ghost of Conn Smythe
haunts the frozen food aisle
of the grocery store on Carlton Street.

He is looking for a secret
pure as sapling springtime.
He knew the answer once:

it smelled of ice.
He knows there were winters here,
beating the snow in the alley

then beating it on the ice.
The ghost of Conn Smythe
is hungry for a miracle:

taps the shoulders of clerks
as they wander in the labyrinth PATH,
watches as bud husks open again

for another sudden death of spring
and fall with no one to catch them
except the wind in the ears

as a streaking winger flies
and salvation shines a red light
and the angel sounds his horn.

The ghost of Conn Smythe
is longing for a place where believing
means the faith of possibility

the way a newborn leaf
means eternity for a maple bough
or at least a moment to live forever.

SECOND INTERMISSION: THE SURLY BONDS OF EARTH

Something was moving through the room. It sounded like the rustling of feathers, and it startled the priest awake.

"Who's there!" he shouted as he switched on the bedside light. He looked around. His books were exactly where he had left them. His slippers were on the floor beside his bed. His typewriter, with the letter half-written to the Prime Minister, squatted neatly on the twist-legged table. A Saskatchewan March wind was still blowing around the corners of the old bank building where he made his home. Everything looked as it should, but he was all by himself.

His eyes fell on the hands of his clock as it ticked patiently on the mantel, and its arms, spread to tell him it was ten to two in the morning, reminded him of Christ hanging on his cross. As he reached to turn out the lamp, he did notice that something was different and tears welled in his eyes.

***

As they crossed the imaginary boundary from Manitoba into Saskatchewan, his son slept in the back seat of the car, curled up with his head on the equipment bag. The level earth stretched off into the horizon and like a sea seemed to calm before them, as if someone had cast bread upon the waters of a storm of rock. He wondered if heaven was a great open space like this. Leaning forward over the steering wheel, he looked up at the open sky. There, he thought, was that blue place of endless possibilities.

His father had served in the Air Force during the Second World War. He remembered the blue uniform that hung in his closet for years, the shoulder visible as he opened the door, and the crested motto beneath the insignia that read *Per Ardua ad Astra: by* hard work to the stars.

"When you are earthbound you learn to reach for the sky." He remembered that from the autobiography of Douglas Bader, the legless Spitfire pilot of the Second World War. He'd read Bader's book and built a collection of model airplanes during the long summer of his twelfth year when they told him he might not walk again, let alone play hockey. He had dreamed of being a hockey player.

His dream for his son was that such a curse would not fall on the boy. Now he had to live his dreams vicariously. But it was worth all the early mornings of 4:00 a.m. practices, the long drives across the prairies to arenas where the coffee machines spewed out brown, undrinkable mud, and where other fathers stood by the boards and relived their youthful dreams through curls of cloudy, hopeful breaths. Heaven, he liked to think, was not just blue, but the wind in his face and the open ice to the goal.

As he passed a gathering of three seed bins that had drawn near the road to watch the traffic pass by, they reminded him of his mother, grandmother and the doctor standing by the door of his room. As they talked in hushed tones like three Fates measuring out the rest of his life, he ran his fingers over the stiff polar landscape of white sheets that made a ghost of his body. He knew that he wouldn't die — spinal injuries don't kill people, the doctor had told him — but something, more than his legs, had gone remarkably numb.

There had been moments in the deepest royal blue over-cloakings of winter dusks when thousands of stars seemed to dance around his head. He felt the rink below him was a ceiling of white cloud, and having risen above it, the rush of wind in his face, he could see the world as God sees it. The scarred ice caught every silver gleam of the one illuminating park lamp, and the blade marks flashed like sabres dueling with his skate blades. That was flying.

When the finality of his injury sank in, he realized that he would never play hockey again. The pictures he had tacked to his bedroom wall, newspaper clippings of Gordie Howe and Jean Beliveau, stared down on him as he lay there. That was the summer before expansion, the summer before Bill Masterton went headlong into the boards during one of the first North Star games. That was a time when players who went down were expected to rise and make their way to the dressing room. The men he idolized were tough, iron men, and to him nothing touched them but their own moments of eternal glory — not their mortality, nor their agony, nor the weakness of their bodies. They never seemed to fall to earth. His glory, like theirs, was frozen in a moment that was over the moment it had happened. A puck crossed the goal line the instant before the red light flashed on. A shot mid-air hovered like a hawk on a dead-calmed updraft as the goalie reached impossibly for it with an outstretched glove. He would regain his legs, but the dreams would skate in someone else's boots. And just when he thought the road would lift him up to heaven and he would soar into the endless blue, the town rose up on the horizon like a goalie coming out to play the angle.

"We're here," he said to his son as the car came to a halt in the parking lot.

***

One winter night during a game, Pere's boys were looking bad. The score was four to one and they were well into the third period. They seemed tired. Their feet lagged behind them as they struggled in the icy air of the rink to catch even a drop of breath to quench the thirst in their lungs. Pere stood on the bench and hollered: "Skate! Skate I say! You'll only get there by hard work. Never lose heart! Skate, you pack of hounds!" And with that, the wind seemed to rise beneath their feet and they won the game five to four. From that moment on, his boys were known as "The Hounds."

Within a few years, the legend of the Hounds had spread throughout the Prairies. The priest's team of vagabonds and needy farm boys had not only built a school; they had built an unbeatable legend. Wherever they played, people came to watch. They watched with awe and admiration. They watched because they saw something in the way the hungry boys played their game as if touched by a divine wind, a spirit that seemed to lift them right off the ice and into the open blue of a Saskatchewan sky. The look in their eyes as they came in on the rush was the look, some said, of avenging angels.

One of those who came to watch and who stayed with the team was a boy of twelve. He wasn't sure what his parents' names had been, where he was born or when. He quickly earned the nickname 'Dreamy' not only because he had a far-away look in his eye, but because his mind always seemed to be somewhere else. He would often walk to the edge of the school's campus on the flat plain southeast of Regina and stare off into the distance across the open expanse where trees lost their height and distances obscured into speculations. He had heard the joke somewhere that a man had watched his dog run away for three days; yet deep down inside his mind as he stood at the edge of his known world he felt he could see forever.

Dreamy became part of the team. He would mutter in his sleep the final score of the next game. His bunk-mates thought it was a joke at first, but when he was correct for the sixteenth time in a row they realized that there was something spooky about him. He had the eyes of someone who was looking not at things but through them. Blue eyes. His gaze was like an open sky.

Through winters when all they had to eat were endless bowls of porridge, Dreamy had looked to Pere as his parent. When the wind blew into the old railway cars that Pere had claimed as dormitories for the boys, the dreamer had taken off his only pair of wool socks and stuffed them in the drafty cracks of the bunkhouse to keep his room-mates warm.

When they had to burn their precious hockey sticks to keep from freezing to death one night when their old truck broke down on the way home from a game, the boy with the sky blue eyes had stood by the priest and prayed that help would deliver them from the sub-zero bite beneath the stars. And as they said their final amen to the prayer, an empty moving van pulled up to the stranded team and their priest climbed into the back.

* * *

Having dropped his son at the Manitoba-Saskatchewan Under-Seventeen tryouts, he decided to stretch his legs, maybe catch some rest before heading into Regina to wait out the hockey camp. The parking lot in front of the Notre Dame Arena was littered with gear — helmets, shoulder pads, shin guards and gloves — as if some epic battle had taken place and the lost warriors had left their armour strewn on the field. The smell of baked sweat rose from the pavement in the boiling midday sun.

This was Notre Dame, the place where God had touched the heart and soul of everything Canadian. As the sign boasted *"Home of the Hounds."* He'd read a great deal about the college and all the famous hockey players who had donned the red and white jerseys of Pere Murray's teams. Wendel Clark, Russ Courtnall, Vincent Lecavalier, Brad Richards were all Notre Dame grads. There was the goaltender, Curtis Joseph, who was often quoted for his paraphrase of something Stephen Leacock was supposed to have said: *The harder I work, the luckier I get.* This was the Notre Dame that a priest and his boys had struggled to build with their bare hands, local charity and a great deal of heart during the hardships and bitter winters of the

Great Depression. It was a place that captured the spirit of Canada's west, the ethic of hard work, honest living, and never-say-die determination.

He looked up from the tumble of equipment and saw a young man walk into a nearby building. The sign on the door read "Visit the Archives." It was a climate cooler inside as the door swung shut behind him. In the centre of the great room, a skylight flooded the space with a heavenly light, and the walls around the aperture were festooned with copies of the Elgin Marbles. The figures were lithe and athletic, young men like the boys at the hockey camp, striving and struggling.

The young man who preceded him into the archives came over and stared up at the marbles with him and after a moment spoke. "When Pere Murray, the college's founder, bought these during the height of the Great Depression, one of his students remarked, 'We don't have enough to eat but you've gone and spent our money on some damned Roman rodeo.'"

"What exactly are copies of the Elgin Marbles doing here in the middle of nowhere?"

"Well," said the young man, "Pere thought they would offer transcendent values. He didn't want his students to live merely by what they saw but by what they could dream. He wanted them to be inspired by great words and deeds and ideas. He wanted them to look up."

"And so we stand here looking up."

"More or less," said the young man. "Take a look around. There's a lot of history here."

The two figures silently wandered from display to display, stopping to peer into the case that contained the books of Robert E. Lee and a tintype of the famous southern general. Another case contained the photograph of a young man in an Air Force uniform.

"Is this one of the students?" he asked.

"He was one of Pere's boys who didn't return from the war. His name was Darren 'Dreamy' Dalton."

The words that the visitor's father had read aloud as a young boy came back to him. "There's a poem. Reagan quoted it when the space shuttle Challenger blew up, but I memorized it as a boy. It was by a pilot named Magee:

> *Oh I have slipped the surly bonds of earth*
> *And danced the skies on laughter-silvered wings;*
> *Sunward I've climbed, and joined the tumbling mirth*
> *Of sun-split clouds — and done a hundred things*
> *You have not dreamed of — wheeled and soared and swung*
> *High in the sunlit silence.*

It concludes:

> *While with the silent lifting mind I've trod*
> *The high untrespassed sanctity of space,*
> *Put out my hand and touched the face of God.*

"That's quite a poem," said the young man. "I've never heard it. You should visit the Tower of God that Pere erected beside the church. It's full of profound sayings that Pere had cast as bronze plaques so they'd survive the ages."

"So, other than the fact that this chap died in the war, why is his picture here in the case?"

"I really don't know," said the young man. "There's a story behind it, but at the moment I really couldn't tell you. It has something to do with a miracle."

"So," he said, turning away from the case, "miracles do happen. Even here?"

The young man simply smiled and disappeared down a back corridor of the archives, evaporating into the recesses of the building, as silently as an eagle hovering over the prairie. It suddenly dawned on the visitor that his guide bore an uncanny resemblance to the airman in the portrait.

***

"Pere," said Dalton as he knocked on the door of the priest's study. "I've got a favour to ask of you."

"What sort of favour? If it is about me benching you this afternoon, all I can say is you've got to keep your feet moving and keep your elbows down when you go into the corners. *All you farm boys love to go into the corners with your elbows up. I'd swear sometimes you were born throwing elbows.*"

The young man laughed. "*No, I didn't mind the point you made. I'm glad you put Frank Germann on today in place of me. If he hadn't been out on my shift we wouldn't have won and my streak of nocturnal predictions would have stopped at seventy-three.*"

"*Pere, I'm here to ask you if you would baptize me.*"

"*Baptize you? Lord sakes Dreamy, you mean to say you were never baptized? Your parents must have seen to that. There aren't many people in this part of the world who wouldn't have their child baptized.*"

"*Well, Pere, that's the point. I don't know what part of the world I'm actually from. I need either a birth certificate or a baptismal certificate in order to prove my age.*"

The priest frowned. "*And why would you need to prove your age?*"

"*Because I want to join the Air Force. They need me. I see very well and they say they need men with good eyesight. I'm quick and strong, and well, I've had these dreams for the longest time that I'm flying. It's strange. I feel as if I am falling, but suddenly I have wings and I'm able to go as far as they will carry me to all the places I've always dreamed of out there on the horizon.*"

"*Dalton, there's a war on. The casualties are high. Do you know what you are committing yourself to?*"

"*A lot more skating into the wind.*"

The priest thought for a moment and then nodded in consent. "*A lot of the other boys are going too. You've worked hard here. Very hard. You should be proud of yourself.*"

"*Pere, the hard work is just beginning. I want to serve my country, but all my life I've had this dream that I could fly up and touch the stars. But in the dream my arms were aching. They were sore from all that flapping and flying. But the dream always ends when I feel the wind in my face and I reach out and I can almost touch them. I think this is the way I can live my dreams. You always told us that we should never give up, that we have to live our dreams.*"

There was a long, silent pause. "*So, Darren, you have no idea of where or when you were born.*"

"*Not a clue.*"

"And you need to prove you exist in order to exist and join the Air Force."

"Yes sir."

"I would talk you out of it, but then if I were your age I'd want to be up there myself. I've always wondered what God looked like up closer. One of these days they'll get me up in an airplane and I'll see for myself."

Pere lit a cigarette that dangled from his lips as he sat entranced in deep thought. "Then there is only one solution." He went to his desk drawer and pulled out a form and began to write on it. "What day would you like to be born?"

"Pardon me?"

"Pick a birth date. Something you can remember in case anyone asks you."

"July 1st. The day Canada was born."

"July 1st it is." Then the priest stood up, went to his desk and poured himself a glass of water. "This should be done with Holy Water, but it is all over in the church and it is too damned cold to walk over there and get it. Right?"

Returning to the young man he stood over him. "Darren Dalton, I baptize you in the name of the Father and of the Son and of the Holy Spirit." He dipped his fingers in the glass of water and made the sign of the cross on the young man's head.

In the months ahead all the boys wrote to Pere and told him of their progress. Some had joined the navy only to discover that they had never swum a stroke in their entire lives. Some joined the army and wrote to their priest about the long marches and endless drills that reminded them of the times they'd walked to Regina. They spoke of their sore feet, and the number of pairs of socks they had been through. Dalton wrote and kept the priest posted on his ascent through the flight schools of the Royal Canadian Air Force.

He had been through the elementary stages on the Tiger Moths, Tigerschmidts they called them on the field. They really weren't more than cloth, wood and wires, but they flew. And he had flown them at a base not far away (he wasn't allowed to name it). Then he had done his service training on Ansons and Harvards at another nearby base before being sent to Ontario for his advanced work on Spitfires. He told the priest how fast the planes were, and how when he was up above the clouds in the endlessness of blue, he thought he could see farther than any vista he had known in Saskatchewan.

One day the priest received a package postmarked Toronto. "Dear Pere," the short note read. "I've had my picture taken. I hope I look scary enough to frighten the Nazi pilots. Best wishes, Dalton."

He held up the picture once it was free of its wrappings. Dalton was scowling. It wasn't the look of someone about to take on a fight, but of someone who had come to a serious doubt about his purpose. It was the look of one who knew he was going down to defeat, not with a sense of defiance but with the overpowering knowledge that there was no way out. He'd seen it on the faces of opposing teams, and he'd seen it once or twice on the faces of his own boys before they rallied. The young man was trying to look like tough stuff. Wasn't that the limit; but was it the truth? He put the picture on his desk and fumbled in his pocket.

He lit a cigarette and his hand shook as he took the picture again and stared into the face of the boy who had always had the eyes of an angel. "Oh Dreamy," he whispered. "Skate, you Hound. Never lose heart."

***

His son was on the ice and the scrimmage was in full flight. The boy took a direct hit on the corner boards and for a moment fell to the ice but picked himself up again and skated down the wing, banging on his chest for wind and back-checking all the way. Just as the other side was changing, an errant pass ended up on his stick and he suddenly reversed the flow. Down the open side he flew and darted into the slot before unleashing a slap shot. The puck soared over the goalie's glove and the mesh behind the back-stopper inflated.

As his son had flown down the wing, he'd felt the rush of wind rise up into the stands, the exhilaration of flying, the endless blue expanse of heaven winging by him in an instant of glory.

"Hey, that kid," said one man with a clipboard to another. They had to be scouts, he thought.

"Yep, he's a keeper," said the other note-taker, as the two men wrote quickly on their pads before looking up to the face-off.

When his son came out of the locker room, his father was there.

"So, you're still here, Dad."

"Thought I'd hang around long enough to watch you pot one. That was some goal." The boy nodded. "Hey, there's something I saw earlier when you were getting ready for the game. C'mon. It's just across the parking lot. This place has a great hockey history and they've made a museum about it."

Within a few minutes they were in the archives. A woman appeared from the office and said, "We'll be closing in a few minutes."

"I just wanted to show my son the picture of the Air Force fellow. It has stayed with me all afternoon since that young guy who works here showed it to me earlier."

The woman looked puzzled. "I don't think there's a young man who works here," she said. "There's only me."

It was then that the picture came to life for him. He stood staring over the case. The young man in the Air Force uniform looked exactly like the boy who had shown him around the archives. And both the picture and the young man bore a striking resemblance to his own son.

**

His eyes fell on the hands of his clock as it ticked patiently on the mantel, and its arms, spread to tell him it was ten to two in the morning, reminded him of Christ hanging on His cross. As he reached to turn out the lamp, he did, in fact, notice that something was different and tears welled in his eyes.

Pere stood up and crossed the room to the wall where he had hung the pictures of the boys who had gone off to the war. He stared hard and long at the dour picture of Darren Dalton. His cap was still tilted slightly to one side with the cockiness of a hockey player looking for a scrap in the corner. The uniform was crisp and correct, "tickety-poo" as he had put it in Air Force language to Pere in one of his last letters. But it was Dreamy's face that was different.

The corners of his mouth were up-turned, the eyes softened and glistened. He was peaceful and angelic. He looked as if he had discovered something wonderful and was waiting to tell everyone. Darren 'Dreamy' Dalton was smiling.

"Sweet Jesus," said the priest. "My boy, my poor boy. I will pray for you." And at that moment Pere Murray realized that Dreamy was dead. He made

the sign of the cross over the young, beaming image, and whispered a blessing as he stood there throughout the rest of the night bearing vigil to the miracle that had occurred.

The eyes in the photograph are full of sunlight, as if the young man has reached up on newfound wings and touched something beyond the stars. As your eyes meet those of the fallen flyer, you can almost feel a soft cool wind dance across your forehead. You can hear a stillness, something more than the silence of that moment just before dawn on the prairie when the sound of starlight filtered through a clear winter night is as profound as those spaces between the words of a prayer.

***

The sky was bright blue and the light was almost blinding. A thunderstorm had crossed the campus town an hour or two earlier and the small puddles were blinding in their reflection and the light stung his eyes. He made the drive back to Regina. He could see the city on the horizon almost every step of the way and it struck him that was how dreams appear to someone who is chasing them — they ride the horizon and the longer it takes to realize them, the slower they seem to grow before the dreamer. He sat in his hotel room with the television's sound turned off and waited for news of whether his son would climb the next step on the hockey ladder. Dreams are hard things to chase. As he surfed through the channels, one in particular caught his attention, not for what was on it, but for what was missing. The channel was blue and empty and reminded him of the Prairie sky.

THIRD PERIOD

THE QUEST

My father took me to see my first hockey game in November of 1968. I was eleven years old, and the NHL had just expanded from six to twelve teams. The new teams were thought to be watered-down versions of the original six, crews made up of castaways who were either too old for the big game or career minor-leaguers who had been raided from the farm teams of the majors.

As the season began, the new teams surprised everyone. They were formidable.

Their strength was a tribute to the depth of original six teams: there were players who had not been given a good look or who had had, as they said in hockey parlance, "a cup of coffee in the NHL" but nothing more. A lot of guys had something to prove. Teams such as Philadelphia and Los Angeles, whose uniforms sported gaudy orange and outlandish purple, suddenly had something to prove. They won games.

The purists, such as my father and grandfather's barber, wanted nothing to do with the new teams. "Who wants to watch Penguins play hockey? And what is one supposed to do about seals?" he'd proffer as he straped his straight-edge on the leather strap.

I was presented with a pair of tickets for Oakland versus Toronto. My father who was not a hockey fan — he had been a judge for the Canadian Figure Skating Association and even into his declining years he could out-mohawk anyone on a rink — knew a man at work who had season tickets in the nosebleed section of Maple Leaf Gardens. Way up in the greys, one row back of an area known as "Standing Room Only" was the location of our seats. They were not really seats in per se, but numbered places on long, hard, punishing, wooden benches, the backs of which rose at ninety-degree angles. I thought I was the luckiest kid in the world.

As we slid into our allotted positions, the first thing I noticed was the absence of the play by play. I was used to Foster Hewitt and then his son Bill Hewitt describing the action on television or radio. I had to watch the play and permit my inner voice to call the game. We were almost too high up to see the numbers of the players' jerseys, but the unmistakeable swoop of Frank Mahovlich or the low stance of Ron Ellis in full flight spoke more than letters or numbers on their backs. The other thing that impressed me was the colour of the uniforms.

Those were the days of the new nylon jerseys and they shimmered under the bright television lights. We only had a black and white television at home so the brightness and the colours impressed me. People shouted things. I thought I should too. I shouted something at Jim Pappin — a very good and underrated player in Leafland — when he missed a pass that could have led to a breakaway.

My father was a quiet, withdrawn man in public. He never shouted things at hockey games. He sat the entire game with his grey fedora on his head, his tweed overcoat buttoned, and his scarf tucked neatly in place. I made him take off his leather gloves so we could share some popcorn.

When the first intermission came, I had to go to the washroom. What greeted me was a kind of communal experience that had not been part of my life up to that point. The urinals were long white troughs, longer than our living room at home. Fathers held their small sons up to pee and old men down the row stood and relieved themselves as if they were cows at a feed bin. I was both repulsed and amazed. Here was a fellowship of men who were kindred spirits, supporters of the blue and white. In a very ancient echo of ritual, we were all united at that trough. I felt a kinship for the huddled masses at the top of the Gardens like I had never felt before.

The final score was Toronto Maple Leafs 3, Oakland Seals 0. Johnny Bower got the shut out. A wrist shot from the slot by former Leaf Kent Douglas clipped Bower over the eye. I remember watching him (through the binoculars of an elderly man down the row who let me have a look) blink through the blood that trickled down his face as he crouched to follow the puck through a maze of legs and bodies. As the arena cleared and everyone went home shouting "Go Leafs Go," I wanted to extract every minute from the experience. We moved along the SRO gangway to middle of the building almost above to centre ice. I did not want to go home.

I stood at the foot of the steps that led up to Foster Hewitt's famous broadcast gondola above the ice. I had seen Hewitt go up there earlier in the game. Jack Dennett, who was the intermission host, came down the steps. Dennett's voice woke me each morning. He was the voice of news on the local radio station my mother listened to. I went up to him. "Mr. Dennett?" I asked. He ignored me.

"Mr. Dennett? Is Mr. Hewitt coming down?"

"Go home kid. Foster left as the game ended," he snarled.

I was crestfallen. I sat there trying to soak in the moment and the fact that I would not meet the man behind the voice I heard late at night as I pressed my ear against the old, overheated bakelite radio in my headboard.

Paul Morris, the arena announcer finished his post-game report on the PA system of the Gardens. At the end of each game, he would provide a recap of the scoring, the penalties, and the number of people in attendance. All these facts would be conveyed the next day in the newspaper. That night, for some reason, he was late getting started with his post-game report. One of the last pieces of information Morris always gave was a small detail that people bet on at that time. They bet on the time of the last goal. The echo of his voice filled the empty seats.

"Time of the last goal was 14:32 of the third period. From everyone at Maple Leaf Gardens, this is Paul Morris wishing you a good night." With that, the bright, white curtained television lights were switched off and the cavernous Gardens fell into a dusky, gloomy silence. It was time to go home.

What has remained with me of that night other than an important time I spent with my father and the sights and smells that I remember from going to my first game was the echo of Morris' voice, the lights suddenly shutting down, and the silence that had filled the vacuum where the roar of the crowd had been heard only minutes before. I was confronted by something devastating, something final and irreversible, a kind of downfall of all the anticipations and excitement I had felt at going to witness a real Toronto Maple Leafs' game. I sat with my father who was anxiously looking at his watch. Where was the redemption of victory?

What I was experiencing was something that Canadians never talk about, the silence and the emptiness after a great event. That silence is our unofficial third language. Only years later would I come to understand what I felt that night when I was eleven as my father and I walked into the cold breath of the night. The streets were raw and glistening with a pathetic late-autumn rain. What I now understand is that despite victory there is something that always comes after the victory that is neither joy nor celebration but the question of "what next," a place where ghosts walk, that realm of our experience we do not acknowledge, a moment when the raw unalterable truth we cannot face always seems too far away to touch.

It is no accident that hockey is one of the great common denominators in Canadian society. When I wasn't dreaming of the Leafs or pushing and shoving with my friends on our driveway or on a dead-end street and pretending we were all Frank Mahovlich, I would don my hockey gear just to feel it next to my body. I could sense the resistance to my movements, the clutch of the gloves on my fingers, and the tight helmet against my forehead. That gear told me I was much more than a hockey player. It said that I was a knight in armour, and my stick was a lance. When I pulled a Leafs jersey over the gear, I felt as if I was the chosen champion of my city.

From the perspective of someone who sits in the stands and watches with awe, hockey players *are* knights. They represent us in what Maple Leafs coach Punch Imlach called "a war on ice." They wear our colours. They represent our cities and our regions. They command our loyalty — a loyalty that borders on a squirely fealty. The most obsessive fans paint themselves in their team colours and parade to the game as if they were the wild, kilted highland men who followed William 'Braveheart' Wallace into battle. Their blood stirs to the sound of the pipes even if that blood does not have a drop of Scottish ancestry. They see themselves as part of a tradition that stretches back in time beyond their births. They are part of a continuum and have taken up the torch to hold high. What we see in hockey and in hockey players is an expression of one of the last vestiges of the Middle Ages. What is also to be seen is the imaginative text that resides at the heart of the Canadian experience. That text is a narrative of Arthurian knights who go on long, hard journeys in order to attain their personal "grail." The eighty game schedule that was introduced in the early Seventies made a single hockey season into a long, machinated quest for victory and a silver cup.

As I pointed out in the introduction, my undergraduate and graduate mentor, the world-renowned literary scholar Northrop Frye, used to stay that if you want to understand a nation and its psyche look at its epics or what it perceives to be its informing imaginative texts. We do not possess the kind of literary expression that defines a nation in the way that *The Epic of Gilgamesh* defines Iraq or the *Chanson de Roland* drove men to perish by the thousands in the mud at Verdun. At first glance, Canada does not appear to have a core text. The United States, however, does.

When the United States was being created by Thomas Jefferson and George Washington, the founding fathers of America had open in front of them two very important works of literature: Virgil's *Aeneid* and Samuel Johnson's *A History of Rasselas: Prince of Abissinia*. From Virgil's *Aeneid*, the American mind drew the principles of nation-building. Americans believe that their president has to be a warrior paragon of responsibility, and possess an almost blinkered moral vision of leadership, though that is one of the first things that is called into question by opposition parties in Congress. Americans live by a principle that I like to call "the Aeneas Factor." Those who have not lived up to the invisible standards, the Aeneas Factor, have been impeached or almost impeached. To underscore the presence of the *Aeneid* as guide-book for nation building, leadership, and the values espoused by republics such as Rome, the founding fathers of the United States went to great lengths to shape their nation around the mythic notion of destiny by geography. This idea of destiny by geography has a number of expressions from Manifest Destiny to the Monroe Doctrine, but the one expression of it that is directly alluded to in the *Aeneid* has become known in literary history as *Troynovant*.

The concept of *Troynovant* or "the new Troy" is quite simple. Toronto even thought it could lay claim to the idea during the 1980s when the term "world class city" was bandied about. According to a prophecy of an oracle that was pronounced prior to the Trojan War, Troy and the Trojan empire is destined to shape the future of the world. Should Troy fall, according to the oracle, the city nation will rise again to the west provided that certain unique geographical features are maintained in the new location. Troy, according to Homer in the *Iliad*, had seven hills with a tower on each hill. A river, the Xanthus, ran through the centre of the city. What the new Troy had to have in order to take its rightful place as the place where the destiny of the world would be determined would be a landscape with seven hills with a river running through it. The location of Rome was determined according to this principle. When Rome fell, the next city to step up to the claim as *Troynovant* was Paris, France. A bit of tinkering with its boundaries in the Seventeenth century, according to Rabelais, provided Paris with what it needed to complete its requisite number of hills in compliment to the Seine. Not to be outdone by the French, the boundaries of London were expanded in 1712 to take in three extra hills; and the sun supposedly never set on the British Empire or, at least, the English language. This idea of a city destined to call the shots on the world is still found in the expression "major league" when it is applied to a city. My Toronto of the 1980s and 1990s wanted to be "major league" or "world class," and the corporatization of the Leafs reflected that desire, especially when the shoulder patch maple leaves were replaced with a stylized trademarked TML. The city, alas, lacked the requisite number of hills, and the two rivers, the Don and the Humber, could not be considered a new Tiber or Xanthus by any stretch of the imagination. Troynovant will never happen in Toronto.

The first capital of the United States was New York, but it was decided early on that it was not a defensible location. Unbeknownst to their countrymen, Jefferson and Washington searched the eastern seaboard for a place that would meet the requirements for greatness. They found a convenient location up the Potomac River, a place surveyed and partially owned by Washington himself, a piece of swampland surrounded by seven hills. Having met the geographical requirements of Troynovant as outlined in the *Aeneid*, America expanded westward and Washington became a "major league" city. The *Aeneid* tells the reader that the greatness of a city resides in the fact that the city has a champion, a knight prince is not both defender and leader — a kind of King Arthur figure who stands above all commoners and is beyond moral reproach. He is Bernard Malamud's Roy Hobbs, the "natural." Christy Mathewson, the early Twentieth century pitcher was such a figure. Hockey has never had such a character and likely will never require one. Hockey is not about moral perfectability off the ice. What Troynovant provides to the Western imagination is not just a sense of political power; what it provides is a home for heroes. If your city is great, everyone in it can or will become a hero. The unending sequel to the *Aeneid* is the Arthurian chronicles. Virgil points out that all of Aeneas' men are knights, and when the *Aeneid* was transformed from a pagan continuum to a Christian one by medieval authors the result was that the heroes of early Rome were reborn as the Knights of the Round Table.

The other text that informed the American experiment was Samuel Johnson's short philosophical novel, *A History of Rasselas: Prince of Abissinia*. If the *Aeneid* provided America with geographical stipulations, then Rasselas gave our friends to the south their values and their ideals of what would be spiritually important to their nation. It is Johnson's *Rasselas* that proclaims the purpose of life as "the pursuit of happiness."

I had no idea how important *Rasselas* was as a founding text for the United States until I was a teenager and my parents took me to see Williamsburg. That small eastern Virginian town is a restored city that is part living demonstration of early American life and part antiquarian show-biz. What fascinated me, more than other things in the restored area was the library of the College of William and Mary. Thomas Jefferson had studied there as an undergraduate and the woman who was the historical interpreter at the library made the mistake of showing me the sign-out book from Jefferson's era. "Here," she announced, "is the signature of the young Jefferson."

"What did he sign out?"

"I don't know. Do you really care?" asked the librarian.

"Yes," I said, "I do care. May I sit down and read through the sign-out book?" I was shown a seat and the book was opened before me as I put on a pair of white library gloves. I was given an hour. As I flipped through the registry, I discovered that Thomas Jefferson kept renewing the same book over and over again throughout his years at William and Mary. The book was Samuel Johnson's *Rasselas*. When I finally got around to reading *Rasselas* I understood why it had fascinated him. The book's main theme is the "pursuit of happiness." The characters never find happiness, but that does not preclude them from chasing it and experiencing all the "ways of life" that are open to an individual. The book is an invitation to practical dreaming.

Johnson was acting as an apologist for the skepticism of David Hume in his short, philosophical novel. Hume questions how we know what we know and states that we cannot be certain of what we witness because every piece of external information has to pass through multiple layers of our perceptual mechanisms in order to be understood. Hume often comes to mind when a referee has to "go upstairs" to the video judge in order to determine the outcome of a challenged goal. Without the use of instant, slow motion replay to dissect an experience as one would at a hockey game, Hume has to surmise that we cannot be certain of what we know. All we can do is to pursue the truth. We cannot really reach it.

Canada's founding texts, however, are from a different era. We missed out on the Age of Enlightenment but came into our own during the Victorian era. We had a revolution of sorts in 1837, but what the uprisings in Quebec and Ontario generated was a sense of reform rather than innovation. Queen Victoria dispatched Lord Durham to investigate the causes of the rebellions (note that the word revolution was not applied), and the results of Durham's Report are still being felt today not only in how we govern ourselves but in how we accommodate our unique imagination where hockey and literature are inextricably woven together. In fact, Durham's Report was part of my History curriculum every year during my high school years. I was constantly reminded, in very subtle ways, that Canada was different from America. I spent years trying to determine why that difference was important. On first consideration, the difference between Canada and the United States had something to do with our use of the letter u in various words and how we make tea, but it was not until the early 1990s that I started to see other differences — and those differences reside in the precepts that Canadians embrace in their constitution. The Americans hold dear the "self-evident truths" of "life, liberty, and the pursuit of happiness." Canadians have enshrined the very legalistic concepts of "peace, order, and good government." And those precepts are the reason why hockey is our game and why I was transmogrified by a parade in April 1962.

When it came time for Canadians to patriate their constitution from England in 1982 and define what it means to be part of the very diverse and vast experience of this country, there were arguments about the nature of our three "self-evident truths." Pierre Trudeau, a philosopher who was informed by the thinking of Thomas Hobbes and Quebec Jesuits, took the stance that Canadians had a right to life, liberty, and the right to security. Trudeau, after all, had been at the helm of the nation during the FLQ Crisis and had invoked the War Measures Act in 1970 to control a "perceived insurrection." Trudeau's trio of values was rejected by the provincial first ministers because his trio of ideals raised all manner of contradictions to existing statutes under Westminster law. What everyone agreed on is an odd trio of fundamental principles, built partly on Durham's Report of 1840 and that document's notion of "responsible government," and partly on the idea that Canadians simply want to get along and live their lives in an anxiety-free state. Anxiety was something we could save for those moments of sudden death overtime in our annual quest for hockey's Holy Grail.

Our constitution now presents our trio of psychological, legal, and imaginative foundations as "peace, order, and good government." What is good is anyone's guess, but the tenets were in keeping with Westminster law. And what was the effect of the new tenets on the Canadian imagination? It may not yet be fully understood, though it is a very poignant commentary not only on who we think we are but on how we are different in so many ways from Americans. We crave the sense of order where life is played by the rules of the game. Happiness, even liberty, are secondary considerations. Order is paramount. Everything else is dispensed at the pleasure of the Crown. 1991's repatriation may have brought the Constitution home to Canada where it could be amended when we require amendments, but it also reinforced Westminster Law — the old traditional ties to motherland Britain that were suggested by the crest on my childhood Eton cap.

The three tenets of the Canadian constitution also suggest why hockey resides at the core of the national consciousness: the game permits us to express our passions in a grand, super-ego forum that is enclosed in wood and glass, played on the most artificial surface in sports, and executed at break-neck speed. All of this bizarre mayhem is refereed both on and off the ice. Offenders are put in a box, just as they were put in a box at the Old Bailey in English justice, and having completed their sentence are permitted to rejoin the play. And what is the purpose of an eighty-game schedule followed by months of playoffs? To win a grail and drink from it in a form of secular eucharist.

Trudeau drew his tenets not merely from his philosophical background but from the literary texts that were open in front of the Fathers of Confederation. As Canada was evolving into a nation the hottest books in the English language were the volumes of Alfred, Lord Tennyson's *Idylls of the King*. Canada and the Canadian game of hockey owes him a considerable acknowledgement.

The legends of Arthur that Tennyson borrowed as the cornerstone for his poems originated in a work by a Welsh monk, Geoffrey of Monmouth in 1138. Monmouth's book, *A History of the Kings of Britain*. Monmouth was attempting to connect Britain to the mythology and continuum of Rome. His work is the source for Shakespeare's *King Lear* and the late romance *Cymbeline*. But more than being a source for Shakespeare, *A History of the Kings of Britain* fuses the motifs and traditions of Virgil's pagan Classical epic, the *Aeneid*, with the stories and motifs of the New Testament. Monmouth transforms the pagan Aeneas into the holy, perfect, Christian knight, Sir Galahad.

When I was five, around the time my passion for hockey began, my grandmother sat me down next to her on her chesterfield and read me *Idylls of the King*. What is intriguing about Tennyson's fascinating rewrites of medieval romance narratives of King Arthur is the impact they had on the culture of Victorian England and its empire. Tennyson argues that the age of Arthur was an age of great faith, an era that saw a tremendous linkage between Christianity and daily life. The knights of Arthur's Round Table were commoners who had accomplished important deeds, overcome great tests and hardships, and proven themselves worthy of sitting down for discourse and meals with a divinely inspired king. Each time I think of the Round Table, I am reminded of my grandfather's front porch, especially the day I came to visit and was greeted by the Prime Minister. Our leaders are commoners. They are among us, not above us. When I worked in downtown Toronto I rode the subway and got to know John Turner. Everytime we met we would discuss hockey. When the playoffs came, we would talk about which team would survive the next round in the process of elimination that leads to a champion.

In *The Quest of the Holy Grail*, a vision of the cup used by Christ at the Last Supper appears in the upper window of the great hall of Camelot and floats through the proceedings as both a vision and an enticement. To a man, the knights of the Round Table decide that they will follow that fleeting vision in order to attain both spiritual redemption in the Christian sense and vegetative redemption for the world from its state of a waste land (what we would call a dead November landscape). Only three knights, Galahad, Percival and Bors, prove themselves worthy of following the grail, and only one, true, perfect knight is able to drink from the Grail as part of a Eucharistic ritual at the climax of the narrative. As Galahad receives the transubstantiated blood of Christ from the cup that was used for the first communion (and which, according to legend, caught the blood of Jesus as he was being crucified), the perfect knight Galahad is conveyed bodily to heaven. I am reminded of the three great knights of the Grail quest when I watch CPAC on television and the leaders of the three parties joust with one another. My American friends have trouble getting their minds around the idea that our government is composed of three very different parties (I often call them the good, the bad, and the ugly), but the concept of a chosen trio of leaders is part of Arthurian quest literature that seems to mean so much to our national psyche.

So, what does all this Arthurian matter have to do with Canada, why are we different from Americans, and why is hockey our game? The answer resides in the fact that at the core of Western literature and the heart of the Western imagination, there are two distinct visions that have tussled for supremacy as the guiding force behind how we perceive the world. Those forces are the Pagan Classical mentality of Greek and Roman literature, a perspective known as "the Ancients," which is set in opposition to the iconography, motifs, dynamics, and principles that inform both the Old and New Testaments of the Bible, a way of looking at the world that has been called "the Moderns." The debate between the Ancients and the Moderns resided at the foundation of the Renaissance when Medieval Christian thought and authority was challenged by a rediscovery of Classical learning. Jonathan Swift in the early Eighteenth century decided to parody the great debate of the Western imagination in his satirical essay "The Battle of the Books."

In terms of how the debate between the Ancients and the Moderns is present in Canada, Northrop Frye, in his film about the Canadian identity, *A Journey without Arrival,* pointed out that Canada missed "the Age of Reason," because "the French and the English were busy battering down each others' forts." Neo-Classical perceptions of a single, noble, Aeneas Factor leadership presiding over a republic form the foundations of American government. Presidents such as Bill Clinton came close to being impeached because they defied the rules of what constituted moral leadership: they broke "the Aeneas code." Canadians are willing to tolerate a latitude of leadership expressions as long as the team, the collective House of Commons, continues to pursue a vision of attainment. We have three commoners who have proven their worth to their parties, and the one whose party gets the most votes runs the national government while two other parties sit in opposition — not antagonism, but in a situation of polite and controlled critique of the government. Galahad, Percival and Bors, the Grail celebrants, are in Ottawa at this moment in what amounts to a tri-party system of assembly.

When it came time for the building of Washington D.C. it is no accident that the city is a collection of Roman temples built around a forum in the manner of the city of Rome. Washington D.C. is situated on a river, and the city is surrounded by seven hills. When the competition to design Canada's Parliament Hill took place, there were two finalists. One finalist, a long, columned Neo-Classical building that looked like a Roman temple with a dome borrowed from the Pantheon in the eternal city was rejected in favour of a structure that was a mixture of Paris' Sainte-Chappelle and a medieval cathedral with a touch of a Loire chateau thrown in for good measure. The age of faith expressed in the architecture of the Medieval Revival was not limited to Parliament Hill.

All over Canada as universities, such as the University of Toronto, grew they designed their campuses from the 1840s on in the shape of castles, baillies, and cathedrals. Most have quadrangles as would castles such as Warwick or Durham. Some, such as University College at the University of Toronto, have cloisters and chapter house. But in the more down-to-earth way, the age of faith made a dramatic appearance in the pointed central Gothic window dormers of Ontario farm houses. Each house, with its church-like window centred over the front door could be a cathedral.

Each home was an expression of faith that, in turn, expressed an order that ran from God to monarch to Man to Nature. The Canadian home was an expression of peace and order, and if Durham's recommendations worked properly, there was good government. Canadians did not want to change their world: they wanted to keep it balanced, they wanted security. World War One upset that notion to the point where the gentility of Canadian society evident in the works of Ralph Connor and Lucy Maud Montgomery lost its relevance as a result of the war.

It is no accident that the rise of professional hockey in Canadian cities such as Toronto coincided with the return of the troops from World War One. Conn Smythe had been an officer. His first CFO was William Barker, the decorated air ace of the Western Front. Hockey provided a controlled emotional outlet for rage, struggle, and the need to pursue victory that had been imprinted on the Canadian psyche during the four years of the war. The soldiers had been, metaphorically speaking, knights-surrogates for Canadian society. In peacetime, they were replaced in the imagination by hockey players.

But there is a more fundamental difference between Canada and America that can be attributed, perhaps, to Tennyson's *Idylls* and *The Quest of the Holy Grail*. What the knights in armour of the Grail stories pursue is a symbol of both spiritual purity and great physical accomplishment. They seek to be champions of what is right and good. They act as our surrogates in the game we are taught to love from childhood. We follow them throughout winter, through our own waste land experience of ice and snow as we sit in our living rooms, dens, or basements and the blue glow from our television sets is cast onto the drifts of snow that surround our houses. The best team survives to win the championship.

And what is their reward? It is not a trophy as one finds in the NFL or Major League Baseball. Americans receive trophies. The World Series Trophy is a miniature ball park surrounded by pennants representing the major league teams. The Lombardi Trophy is a football mounted on a triangular plinth. They are symbolic of victory, most certainly, but they serve no other purpose than to commemorate victory. Canadians in their quest for sports glory pursue cups: the Grey Cup, the Memorial Cup, the Allan Cup, and above all, the Stanley Cup. As is the case with the three

Grail supplicants who receive the blood of Christ in the climax of the Grail story, Canada's champions drink spirits (champagne) from a chalice that symbolizes both the victory and the agony it took to achieve that moment of supremacy. When I finally took myself to the Hockey Hall of Fame with my daughter and nephew in tow about five years ago, I approached the Cup chamber with great reverence. I had the feeling that I was Sir Bors, the knight who would receive the grail and then return to write about it. That room has a profound sense of secular holiness about it. The cup is surrounded by the portraits of those who have been inducted as members of the Hockey Hall of Fame. Their ghosts and shadows are the chosen guardians. They are the former warriors of seasons past.

And so, as the ice melts and it is almost too hot outside on a June evening to keep the playing surface solid inside the arena, the champions shed their helmets and their gloves and raise the cup. They stare into the television cameras full of joy and bearing the visible scars of their struggles — including medieval-looking playoff beards. And as they drink from the Stanley Cup, the entire nation bears witness to the conclusion of the hockey season with a celebration of a secular eucharist. For their efforts, the players and the coach receive a small token of redemption and everlasting life when their names are engraved on the cup eternal.

THE PARADE

Coming home on a winter afternoon,
my mind always drifts into twilight.
Beneath the glow of a January moon
I see three boys playing in a street

and know time can slow and linger
the way a snowflake lives forever
the instant it melts on my finger.
Their sticks are raised in the air.

They shout to heaven with a roar
of inspiration curled from each lip,
and everything they reach for
is there like snow on my fingertip.

Forever is a long time to dream of.
A shot leaves my blade and wings
into that moment where only love
and anticipation can bring

it home. My arms fall like snow.
Can I touch the stars before time runs out?
Will I have another shot tomorrow?
Is this a dream where I cannot shout?

They shout to heaven with a roar
of inspiration curled from each lip,
and everything they reach for
is still as snow on my fingertip.

SUDDEN DEATH OVERTIME

ARENT ARENTSZ'S "SKATERS ON THE AMSTEL," 1625

Far in the distance where eternity
fades into the memory of sunlight,
a skater with a hockey stick
winds up to aim his blast at you.

You are Time's goalie. You wait
for the shot that never comes,
peering through a forest of legs
because you are a brave keeper,

keeping watch upon a morning
when the canal froze over
and you ran like wild Christmas
to skate in the path of winter

leaving your mark etched in ice
as if it was a hero's autograph
that you'd treasure to the end
where no one can put it by you.

TIME OF THE LAST GOAL

In the Art Gallery of Ontario there is a painting that dates from 1625 by the Dutch artist Arent Arentsz. It is a canal scene in winter. The water has frozen over and about eighty or more figures are out on the ice, much like the people who skate in Nathan Philips Square in front of Toronto's "new" City Hall. Everyone in the painting appears to be having fun.

About center in the canvas, there is a young man with what looks like a curved branch from a tree. He is not using the branch for support. Instead he appears to have a black, round, disc-like object in front of him and he is winding up to take what appears to be a slap shot. He is aiming the puck directly at the beholder. The puck, if the shooter ever makes contact with it, will fly out of the canvas and strike the viewer of the future between the eyes. When I saw "Skaters on the Amstel" for the first time and realized that the shooter was there, taking aim at me, I wanted to crouch in a goalie stance. Alas, art and time stand between me and the shooter and that is a small tragedy. I know I could stop him if I could get into the painting to cut down the angle. Even if the idea is merely a fanciful conceit, Arentsz does bring out the goalie in those who look carefully at the work of art.

Most people walk by or away from Arentsz's painting without noticing that there is one figure on the canvas who is trying to play hockey. That is a shame because in that minute detail, the painter is telling us that we are all goalies. In the modern rendition of hockey, we would be wearing masks to keep our faces intact. We would be hiding behind the *persona* — the image that the mask projects to frighten the shooter. Goalies such as Gilles Gratton painted their masks to look like the heads of tigers roaring back at the shooter. I admire goalies more than any other players on the team. Their purpose in the game and perhaps their purpose in the world is to stand up and defy what is coming at them and stop it. Goalies, like questing knights are weighed down in body armour and their chief purpose is to save us from defeat and redeem us for victory. They stand on guard.

In 1998, not long after I got out of Al Smith's taxi cab, he took $34,000 of the money he had received in the settlement between lawyer Alan Eagleson and the NHL Players Association, and invested it in one of the oddest, perhaps least expected literary adventures Canada has known. Eagleson had cheated the players out of millions of dollars in their pension fund. The eventual settlement was a hard-fought battle led by a member of the 1962 Toronto Maple Leafs, Carl Brewer. Al Smith decided, after leaving hockey in 1981 and bouncing around a number of jobs and positions, that he would drive taxi and write in his spare time.

Having penned an autobiography which he self-published, a little-known volume titled *The Parade Has Passed*, he became fascinated, as was evident the day of our conversation, with the idea of tragedy. His play, *Confessions to Anne Sexton*, was produced by the Alumnae Theatre in Toronto. Only seventeen people witnessed the production, and poet and theatre critic Kevin Connolly remarked that he felt badly for the former goalie because there appeared to be more people on the stage than in the audience. The play closed after twenty-one performances and for the majority of those performances, no one showed up to watch.

Confessions to Anne Sexton was an intriguing idea, perhaps a brilliant idea that was presented to an audience that did not possess the ability to understand what it was witnessing or could witness. What was presented on stage was an attempt to create a Canadian tragedy.

A WHA goalie, "Little" Bill Henry, has an epiphany about the meaning of life one night in 1977 while trapped in Buffalo during a blizzard. Thirteen years later Henry hooks up with a character that Damien Cox described as "a corporate hot shot," and the goalie attempts to explain the meaning of life to his friend as they travel to Boston to see an exhibition by the late-Impressionist painter, Eduoard Vuillard. During the course of their road trip, the former goalie tries to understand why his life fell apart. I have not been able to locate a copy of the play. The Alumnae Theatre never kept a script. The director misplaced his copy years ago. Presumably, it is lost forever.

The title, however, does evoke the conversation I had with Smith. Sexton and Plath, two of the most tragic figures of Twentieth century poetry studied together for only a month in a workshop at Cambridge,

Massachusetts, run by another tragic figure of American poetry, Robert Lowell. After the workshop, Lowell, Plath and Sexton went their separate ways though all three followed similar destinies. All three attempted suicide. Lowell survived to die of a heart attack in the back of a New York taxi cab in 1977, approximately around the same time as "Little" Bill Henry's epiphany. So what was the epiphany? What was that knowledge that Smith came by through hardship and suffering and the ups and downs of life as a professional goalie? Why did he title the play *Confessions to Anne Sexton*?

At the time of his death from pancreatic cancer in 2002, Smith was working on a tragic novel, *The Tragedy of Lake Tuscarora*. Why was he enamoured with tragedy? Perhaps as a goalie, he had spent his entire professional career, at least from the moment he left the Maple Leafs, behind a goalie mask. The mask in theatre is called a *persona* (the adoption of an expression of a character's condition frozen on his face rather than the expressive gesturing of a character's experiences and reactions). The persona is one of the elements that still remain part of drama from Classical tragedy. Every actor dons a mask to become a character even if he or she is not wearing a physical mask. The actor is speaking to the audience through an identity that he or she assumes. The voice of the speaker (not necessarily the author but the speaker that has been created to convey the information in a piece of literature) is also called a persona. You have been listening to a persona throughout this book who has been telling you stories and expressing thoughts about the role of hockey in the Canadian imagination.

One of the works I discuss with my students as a means of an entrée into an understanding of how the literary imagination functions is *The Poetics*, a handbook to creative writing, tragedy, and epic poetry that Aristotle created for his students around the time of Alexander the Great. In Classical tragedy, according to Aristotle in *The Poetics*, there are six elements that go into the experience of the play: plot (what happens), character (who it happens to), thought (the philosophical reaction to one's condition expressed as a statement of what the character learns from suffering), diction (the language of the play that is elevated almost to the level of unfigurative religious expression), spectacle (the witnessing of the event), and song (the element in the language of music that is an expression of the ritual at the core of the action). As dramaturgy dictates, Smith was trying to achieve these elements in his play. The problem for Al Smith may have been that his art was speaking to the wrong audience. Those "ancient-minded" Americans probably would have understood, but the "modern-minded Canadians" could not see the point of tragedy. In the modern mentality, there is no catastrophe. As bad as things get, there is always the possibility of redemption. This fact alone explains why there is one thing that is missing in Canadian literature. Tragedy. Why is Canadian literature devoid of tragedy.

The answer may reside in the very imaginative foundations of our national psyche that makes hockey so important to us. In the Modern or Judeo-Christian mentality of Western literature, the reader is faced with the constant assertion that tragedy is impossible because God is in his heaven, all is right with the world, and all things are governed by the power of a force called Providence where God's plan is slowly revealed. Shakespeare is aware of the fact that his plays are being played before an audience of Moderns, and solves the insinuation that God is dead by relocating his tragedies in the Pagan-Classical universe. Shakespeare achieves this by making God lower-case, small g "gods." In the Judeo-Christian universe, anyone who goes with the providential plan, according to the Roman philosopher Boethius in *The Consolation of Philosophy*, is good. Even if a person suffers terribly, he will eventually be redeemed as long as he maintains his faith in God. Those who opt out of the order of God and Nature, according to Boethius, are evil. The evil are punished for actively working against the forces of good. Canadian literature embraces the redemptive aspects of human experience. The characters often suffer mightily, but in the end they find meaning, purpose, a vision or an epiphany that rescues them from total despair. That little gothic window in the dormer of farmhouses is actually a lens through which we see the world. And the world, no matter how bad it gets, belongs to characters who endure with a Job-like determination not to curse God and die.

American literature, on the other hand, comes from a different category of imaginative foundation. American literature is built upon the ideas of Classical literature. In Classical literature there is tragedy. Heroes fall and they suffer. When a hero is defeated the audience suffers with him. There is a communal catharsis, a sharing of spontaneous grief. Certainly, there are the O. Henry stories where characters pull themselves up by their bootstraps and overcome the odds, but that pursuit of happiness is little more than what Bertrand Russell categorized as "Logical Positivism," the pursuit of wealth and material prosperity exemplified by Jay Gatsby — the pursuit of transitory "things." Boethius warns against material prosperity because, in his words, it is all an illusion of happiness and not real happiness. A person can pursue happiness as much as they want, but in the end it doesn't really mean anything. In Canadian literature there are no Jay Gatsbys and there are no Willy Lomans. The Canadian psyche would not permit it because the nature of tragedy defies the existence of a loving God with whom communion can be taken in moments of triumph. The "tomorrowness" of hockey, especially for those who have watched generations pass between Stanley Cup victories, suggests that the possibility of redemption is always there if one is willing to have faith long enough to see the foretold victory become a reality. This is consolation to a person such as myself who is still waiting to stay up late and watch my team win next year.

In his essay on tragedy, "Death of a Salesman," written in 1948 to accompany his tragic masterpiece *Death of a Salesman*, Arthur Miller comments that tragedy in the Twentieth century has relocated itself from being the pastime of the high-born, the *spoudaios*, and is now a universal phenomenon shared by the masses, the low-born *phaulos*. Hence, Miller's protagonist is named Willy Loman. The first name, Willy, is the key to the way the audience perceives the protagonist. Will he overcome the odds and succeed in the face of impossible challenges or will he suffer a catastrophe, a reversal of fortune, and the inevitable downfall afterwards? The last name suggests that Willy is a common man, and that tragedy is now a shared, democratic experience, a malady of the masses.

Tragedy is full of suspense, but it is not the suspense of a seventh game sudden death overtime. In tragedy there are no winners to lap the rink with the cup. In hockey, there are. A fan goes to a hockey game knowing one thing is inevitable (at least under the current NHL format that forbids ties): someone is going to go home a winner either via overtime or via a shootout. What is intriguing about the NHL winner rule that was introduced only a few years ago is that it says that hockey cannot be tragic. There will be a losing team, but there will also be a winning team.

The troubling aspect in this discussion is not that tragedy seems to be missing from Canadian literature, but that tragedy is one of the hallmarks of a mature literature. Missing from the Canadian canon is a *Moby Dick*, that encyclopedic novel that offers a meek and almost thanatically allusive redemptive conclusion — Ishmael floating on the coffin of a dead shipmate.

Perhaps Al Smith was attempting to challenge something in our psyche. Perhaps, through the eyes of the persona of his trade, he saw something that needed to be challenged but struggled to find a way to make that challenge acceptable on literary terms. Or, perhaps he was caught up in the literature of the other side of the border, a prisoner of its powerful ethos. As Damien Cox notes in his book *67*, a work about the Leafs' last cup, Al Smith had been rushed to the Gardens to serve as back up to Terry Sawchuk after Johnny Bower was injured in warm-up. He was part, but not completely part, of the last great miracle on Toronto ice. Smith watched from the bench as Sawchuk won the game; but what if goalie-Al had gotten into the game? His name would have been on the Stanley Cup. Even in the WHA the sip from the AVCO Cup eluded Smith. The tragedy was not the play he was trying to write or the novel he left unfinished but the fact that he never won a championship. He looked into the slapshot that had inevitable defeat written all over it and knew he could not stop it. Rather than pounce on the loose puck and freeze it, he chose to play it. I have the sense that winning a cup meant something to Al Smith, but I will never know. In Smith's case, the rest is silence.

Canadian literature, in fact the Canadian identity, is founded on the presence of silence. Silence is our third, though unofficial, language. So much resides in what we do not say — the unbearable universal truths that are heard in great and powerful truth that Americans utter in the profound tragic speeches of Miller and Eugene O'Neill — truths that we fail to realize we are not hearing. I heard that silence at the first game I attended. Toronto 3, Oakland nothing. It was the absence of someone to explain things. Tragedy, in the Xlassical sense, is all about trying to explain why bad things happen to heroes. The tragic hero, such as Oedipus faces the audience and shares what he knows. Tragedy for all its shock and horror teaches and enlightens. And when they turned out the lights on the Gardens and Paul Morris said goodnight at the end of his recap and announced the time of the last goal, what I heard was that voice of silence and I was afraid because I could not understand what it was trying to say, and I am still afraid because the literature I live in has not been able to teach me how to know what it is saying.

Hockey is not a game that we chose as a nation: it is a game that chose us. We didn't invent it. It attached itself to us because of our unique national foibles. It is the expression of our history and how we have chosen to wrestle with our own peculiarities. Hockey is played all over the world, and Canadians have been the game's greatest evangelists. As Arentsz's painting suggests, the sport has been around a lot longer than our country. There are many things that can be said for hockey: it is a game of speed; it is a sport of determination, skill, and strength; it is a pastime of dreams and imaginings, and as a result we are such stuff as dreams are made on. It has become, in many ways, a corporate spectacle, a cash cow, and a jaded activity. That may be true on the professional level. But when I was on the train journey I describe in the poem "Road Hockey," I did wake suddenly from a dream and the first thing I saw through the blowing snow hurtling past the passenger car window was a cross-road where three or four boys were battling for the puck around a portable goalie net. Out of nowhere the game spoke to me as I remembered it. In that moment, hockey reminded me why it is our national sport: it is a form of protection — not quite an expression of comfort — but a buffer we draw around ourselves that says we are armed and armoured against the bleak, stark finality, the loss of hope, and the crushing sense of defeat that is found in nations that embrace and express tragedy. That brief vision of play was a reminder that we still have heroes we cheer for and that they are our champions, our surrogates in the action, our knights in body armour. Perhaps Canada is still clinging to a form of naievty where we want to believe that everything will work out for the best, that there will be a winner this year, and that next year is a whole new season that could be *our* season, *our* moment of glory. All sports work on the principle of hope, but hockey, especially Canadian hockey, is built out of the symbols and metaphors of the quest for eternal life and redemption.

When we were young and playing road hockey on my parents' driveway or on the little-traveled crescent across the way, we called the plays as we went. We narrated our experience because we wanted to project ourselves into the shapes and shadows of our heroes. It was not just a game but a story we were trying to tell ourselves where we were the champions. And no matter what the real score was, we never went home feeling as if we had lost. Every day was the day we raised our cup. Daily, on dead-end streets and neighbourhood driveways with pock-marked garage doors, we enacted the ritual fantasy that was within our grasp. We were Gordie Howe. We were Frank Mahovlich. We were Johnny Bower. When one of us scored, someone would shout "instant replay" and in slow motion we would re-enact the goal that had just been scored, complete with play-by-play and colour commentary. We dreamed of being hockey players. We lived, breathed, and dreamed hockey.

It was our religion. We were its humble vassal knights, sworn to chase a dream that none of us would ever reach. When we went to hockey schools on outdoor rinks on those snowy nights when the sky settled on our miniature uniforms of the Leafs and the Canadiens, we dressed in our armour — shoulder pads, shin pads, gloves, and helmets. We donned our gear as if we were arming for battle or a long quest where we would have to prove ourselves, though few of us could stand up for long in our skates as our rubber ankles stretched beneath us. None of us knew that we were arming ourselves for the quest of our own futures, and none of us knew that our hockey dreams would come to naught. We had sworn a vow to ourselves. We would pursue that infinite moment of glory. We would die trying to achieve it and be the one who marked the time of the last goal.

We would run home from school and gather at the local rink in a park not far from home where the home-owners association had set up splintery boards and flooded the grass each morning. We would skate and skate and shoot and struggle until the stars came out and our mothers would drag us home half-frozen for the needles of a hot bath and the beautiful sensation of a re-warmed dinner. And in our dreams as our days faded before us into sleep, we would dream that we were raising the Stanley Cup above our heads.

One night, after the others had gone home, I skated alone beneath the stars. My breath was caught in the still, silent winter air before me, and it hung there as if a vow that I felt I had to uphold. The snow had hardened on my wool Maple Leafs jersey and I clutched my stick and stared at the one, lone net that sat at the far end of the rink. I wanted to score the winning goal. I wanted to put my mark on the silence of my world. I wanted to be the one who would attain the Grail by scoring the last goal.

And as it was in the night of my first hockey game at Church and Carleton, in the silence that followed the moment when Paul Morris announced the time of the last goal to the echoing emptiness of Maple Leaf Gardens, I recognized what is possible and what remains to be discovered in who and what we are as a people and as a nation. Our voice and our vision have yet to be completely born as an imaginative force. But I also see an invitation in that announcement: an invitation to a quest. The goal that we seek is still out there hovering like a grail before our eyes if only we can see it. I am as certain that we will find what is great within us as I am that next winter and the winter after that and for winters to come there will be boys and girls chasing a puck or a frozen ball with the aim of writing their name on a goal. As a hockey fan, I am always certain that next year will be the year. When it comes we will seize the cup and hoist it above our heads so it almost touches heaven.

ACKNOWLEDGEMENTS

The author would like to thank Terry O'Malley, former president of Notre College in Wilcox, Saskatchewan for his help with information, and Karen Wetmore of Grenville Printing at Georgian College for her assistance with the processing of the visuals. And a special thanks to Marty Gervais and Jason Rankin of Black Moss Press for their great support and ideas during the evolution of this book.

"I Say the Walls Shall Crumble Down" appeared in *The Windsor Review*.

"Skating" has not been previously published in English. The story appeared in an edition of 750,000 in China in the journal *Flying* at the University of Lanzhou.

"The Surly Bonds of Earth" appeared in *In the Dark: Canadian Ghost Stories*, edited by Myna Wallin and published by Tightrope Books.

ABOUT THE AUTHOR

Bruce Meyer is author of over forty books of poetry, short fiction, non-fiction, pedagogy, and literary journalism. He is the inaugural Poet Laureate of the City of Barrie where he teaches college and university, and lives with his wife and daughter. His broadcasts on literature, including those on the Great Books, have been heard on the CBC and are the network's bestselling spoken word series.